Careers in Anthropology

SECOND EDITION

John T. Omohundro
State University of New York, Potsdam

Mayfield Publishing Company
Mountain View, California
London • Toronto

Library of Congress Cataloging-in-Publication Data

Omohundro, John T.
    Careers in anthropology / John T. Omohundro.—2nd ed.
       p. cm.
    Includes bibliographical references and index.
    ISBN 0-7674-1861-1
    1. Anthropology—Vocational guidance. I. Title.
GN41.8.O56 2000
301'.023—dc21   00-060543

Manufactured in the United States of America
10   9   8   7   6   5   4   3   2   1

Mayfield Publishing Company
1280 Villa Street
Mountain View, CA 94041

Sponsoring editor, Janet M. Beatty; production editor, Julianna Scott Fein; manuscript editor, Mary Ray Worley; design manager and cover designer, Jean Mailander; art editor, Rennie Evans; text designer, Anne Flanagan; illustrator, Emma Ghiselli; manufacturing manager, Randy Hurst. The text was set in 10/13.5 Garamond Light by Archetype Book Composition and printed on acid-free 50# Thor Offset by Malloy Lithographing, Inc.

 This book is printed on recycled paper.

Preface

This workbook can be used by students on their own, or with their advisors, or as part of a group assignment, either in a workshop setting or as a course supplement. In our department, all new anthropology majors receive a copy to work through. Many of our introductory students and all senior anthropology major students are expected to read it. I'd be pleased to correspond with instructors about teaching with this book (omohunjt@potsdam.edu).

Inevitably, some Web pages cited herein will change addresses or be eliminated in the next few years. I maintain a Web site of up-to-date links and new careers sites at *www.potsdam.edu/anth/careers/latestLinks*.

NEW TO THIS EDITION

This second edition of the workbook was inspired by students and colleagues who enthusiastically welcomed the first edition and suggested items to include. It was also forced by the happy fact that there has been an explosion of information about career development for anthropology students, on the Internet as well as in print.

Chapter 3, on the careers of professionals, has been completely rewritten to update the examples and to sketch the careers of three professional anthropologists. Chapter 6 is expanded, with more alternatives for graduate school as well as a timetable for planning. Chapter 7 is expanded with profiles of the careers of five anthropology majors and a flow chart of career decisions. There are two new exercises. Exercise 14 offers advice on how to read and respond to job ads. Exercise 15 uses a questionnaire technique to sharpen one's self-understanding. Other exercises are revised based on experience in my classes. Overall, there are more sources, including many Internet sources, and much information is updated.

ACKNOWLEDGMENTS

Thanks are due to the many who participated in the workbook's evolution from a stapled stack of dittoed sheets to this revised edition. Steve Marqusee, my department chair, cotaught the prototype of this workbook with me in the anthropology senior seminar and continues to teach the seminar using this book, passing on more ideas. Karen Johnson-Weiner has given me a broader picture of what linguists can do. Ellen Kintz shared her career advising resources, as did Jim Armstrong and Karen Szala-Meneok.

Hundreds of undergraduates have field-tested the exercises. They and their professors have offered a number of suggestions. Glenn McRae should be singled out. The eight people profiled in Chapters 3 and 7 have paused in their busy day to revise my summaries of their interesting careers. More than a dozen other anthropology degree holders provided guidance in composing the short profiles of their work. Jan Beatty of Mayfield took a chance on the first edition of this workbook and then sensed when it was time to bring the topic up to date again. Julianna Scott Fein skillfully saw this second edition through production.

My perspective on careers has been shaped by Jim Barrick, past director of Career Services at SUNY College at Potsdam. It's been an eye-opening professional collaboration.

Contents

EXERCISES

Introduction

FIRST AID FOR "ANTHRO SHOCK"

The following scene happens at least once a semester: A distraught student pokes her head through my office door.

"Excuse me. . . . Are you busy? I need to ask you something."

"No, Grebbleberry, come in— sit down. What's bothering you?"

"I really like anthropology. In fact, I want to drop my major in [deleted] and declare in anthropology, but when I told my parents, they were freaked out. My mother cried, and my father threatened to cut me off, and my friends think I've lost it completely. Now they've got me scared. I'm afraid I won't be able to get a job. What am I going to do?"

This student has all the symptoms of *anthro shock*. If I even crack a smile, I've lost her.[1] This is *not* a laughing matter. For immediate first aid, I give the easy answer to alleviate the panic the student is feeling, which may be summarized as "mocked and alone, I'm going to starve." Firmly, I say,

> Take courage. There are many things you can do for a living that will utilize your anthropological knowledge and skills. I can help you discover them and prepare for them.

Only then does the student's color begin to return; the anthro shock is in remission. Later, perhaps, after we've got her career development program under way, I might introduce the difficult answer. The difficult answer, so called because it is difficult for students to believe, goes something like this:

---

[1]Grebbleberry is female because more than half of my advisees are women; however, many male students also come to me with anthro shock.

1

For most careers, it doesn't matter much what you major in, as long as you like the subject and are good at it. The point of a liberal arts education is to gain practice at studying something in depth. One's major is not the same thing as job training. The careers that follow from most undergraduate majors are not and cannot be specified, even if the world doesn't change—which it does, frequently. There is no direct, obvious, and inevitable connection between college disciplines and the occupational titles people acquire. (See the box titled "What Were Their Majors?")

Although everything I've learned in the past twenty years of career counseling convinces me that the difficult answer I've just described is true, it's likely that Grebbleberry still won't believe me, because it goes against everything pundits, peers, parents, and some professors tell her.

Ah, well. If quantitative data impress you, then examine Figure 1, which indicates that over the last twenty years the number of students getting degrees in anthropology has increased nearly 300 percent. Do these students know something you don't?

Through "hard" facts and exercises, this workbook emphasizes two main points: (1) undergraduate students can find good positions that use their

---

What Were Their Majors?

Here are several occupational titles held by recent Potsdam College graduates. In the blanks, write the major you think the student completed in college. Answers are on page 150.

Banking assistant manager   _____

Child disability learning specialist   _____

Physical education center instructor   _____

Conservation agent   _____

Stock market analyst   _____

Newspaper reporter   _____

Paralegal professional   _____

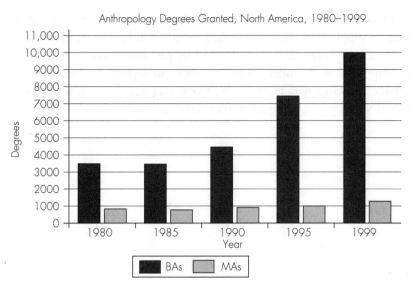

FIGURE 1   Anthropology Degrees Granted, North America, 1980–1999. Data from
Guide to Departments of Anthropology.

anthropology, and (2) they can use their anthropology to find those positions.
The workbook provides exercises that will enhance the undergraduate student's confidence, efficiency, competitiveness, and resourcefulness in getting
educated and finding work related to anthropology. It will also teach students
some anthropology, because to work with this book is to adopt the anthropological perspective on the job-getting process. The exercises also introduce
several anthropological field techniques for students to practice.

I also repeatedly illustrate two subordinate themes. First, how one gets
from college to satisfying work is a function of one's entire life experience,
the complete range of one's talents and interests—not just what one's major
was. Second, much of what needs to be done to find good work is not usually included in the liberal education curriculum. Finding good work is like
enrolling in an "independent study" course that no one said you had to take
and that few people feel competent to teach. But, oh, the satisfaction you'll
gain from passing that course!

Students at any level of anthropological study will find this workbook
useful. The beginning student curious about the discipline and pondering
what to major in will benefit most at this time from reading Chapters 1, 3, and
4 and performing the associated exercises. The newly declared major, who is
trying to figure out how to explain anthropology to others, what one needs

to learn as anthropology major, how to select a career, and what to study in college to supplement the anthropology major, will benefit most at this time from reading Chapters 2, 5, 6, and 7 and by performing the associated exercises. The advanced student thinking about attending graduate school or about seeking employment in the next year will want to turn to Chapters 6, 7, 8, and 9 and to complete the associated exercises.

CHAPTER 1

"You're Studying *Whaat*?"

How to Explain Anthropology to Others

For twenty-five years I have had to explain to relatives, friends, and seat-mates on airplanes what it is that I do. I'm getting pretty good at it. I need to be. Anthropology is widely misunderstood. You will have to make an effort to explain yourself to others. A survey of college students who hadn't taken an anthropology course found that almost all students knew what psychology and geology were, but a fifth had no idea what anthropology was. Most of the others thought it was about "bones and stones," which is partially correct. Only about a fifth even mentioned "other cultures" (Bird and Von Trapp 1999). Less than one-fifth of all students could name three jobs that someone with a B.A. in anthropology could fill. Many thought a career in fast food was an anthropology student's only option!

Anthropology is misunderstood not only by parents and friends but by personnel officers of government agencies (Givens 1986) and chairs of departments in other disciplines (Bronitsky 1999). Fortunately, the ignorance gap is closing as more anthropologists take positions in government and business, appear on television talk shows, and in other ways get the word out.

Looked at from an ethnolinguistic point of view, the presentation of one-self as an anthropologist—whether to informants in the field or to parents and employers—is a translation process. I tailor my answer to my listener's interest and education. I make it as easy as possible for my listener to understand and respect me by putting what I know into categories that can readily be grasped and appreciated. In communication theory, that's called improving my "indexicality" (see Figure 1.1). Here are some examples of my replies. If you love anthropology, start practicing your own replies.

What is anthropology?

My answer: Anthropology is the scientific study of humankind, in all times and places, using comparative methods. It's made up of four subdisciplines: linguistics, cultural anthropology, archaeology, and bio-logical anthropology.

Write your answer in the space following this paragraph. Then memorize it and practice it in front of a mirror until your demeanor says, "I know what I'm doing."

What is cultural anthropology?

My answer: Cultural anthropology is a social science whose practition-ers try to understand and explain humans by living in and comparing their cultures.

Your answer:

So, what is culture?

My answer: Culture is the set of understandings that a group of people share about how to behave and about what everything means.

Your answer:

Exercise 1, ""Ethnosemantics," at the back of this workbook, helps you to indexicalize your answers by clarifying through anthropological research just what people think anthropology is.

Your development of the anthropological skills introduced in this work-book will actually help you gain employment. Suppose you are sitting in the office of the director of the museum where you want an internship this sum-mer. The director looks at your résumé and smiles, "Anthropology? We don't do digs."

What do you say? Jot down the reply that will most likely ensure that you are taken seriously as a candidate for this internship:

Does your explanation offer a broader conception of anthropology and mention some of the ways it could be valuable in a museum setting? Explaining yourself as an anthropology major to a potential employer, as you just did above, is very similar to explaining yourself to hosts and informants when you are beginning ethnographic fieldwork. Both situations boil down to tests of your transcultural communication skill: knowing the listeners' world, knowing your own, and then making a convincing translation that increases their respect for and trust of you. Exercise 12, "Interview Yourself," and Exercise 13, "Building Rapport with a Potential Employer," are necessary practice for the advanced student to develop this transcultural communication skill.

Ann Thropologist, Ph.D.
Cultural Anthropologist

Box 123   Cross-cultural Research
Laramie,   Human Sexuality
Colorado 82345   Myth, Ritual, and Symbol
                                 Corporate Culture
(303) 345-6789   American Society

Research Design and Analysis
Focus Group Moderation and In-Depth
Interviews
Cross-cultural Communication and Training
Organizational Evaluation and Development

Ann Thropologist, Ph.D.
Cultural Anthropologist

Box 123, Laramie, Colorado 82345
(303) 345-6789

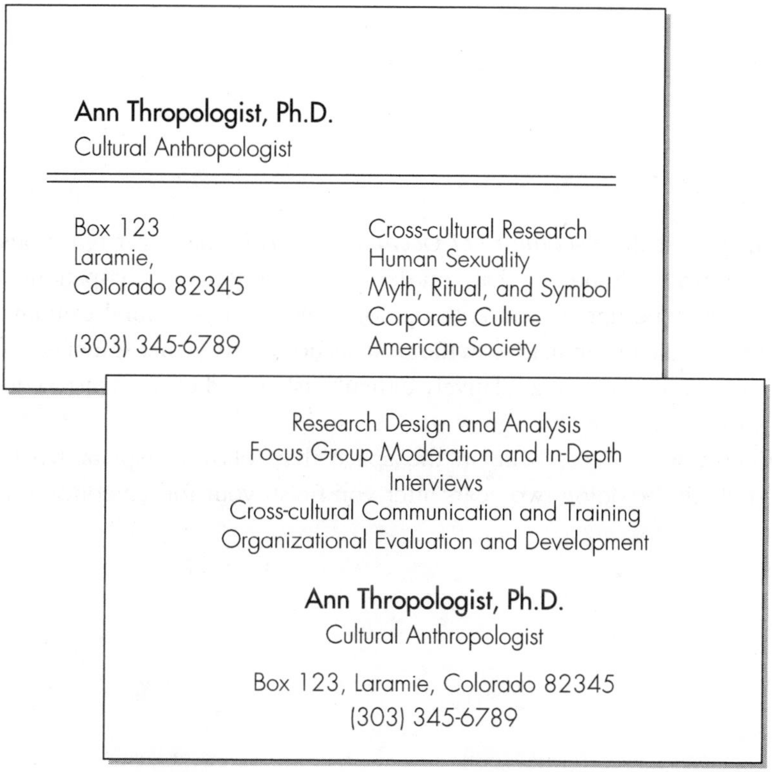

FIGURE 1.1   Indexicalizing Your Anthropology. This independent professional has one business card for colleagues, one for nonanthropologists.

Career Education from the Anthropological Perspective

Begin with a self-test. In the following spaces, list all of the occupations you understand from firsthand experience—that is, you've done them yourself or you've followed others who do them.

1.

2.

3.

4.

5.

6.

Given that the *Dictionary of Occupational Titles* has over ten thousand entries, I can safely predict that you don't know very many occupations. This situation may be understood anthropologically. A cross-cultural examination of careers, which I summarize in the next section, reveals that students in contemporary America have a relatively difficult task ahead of them just to decide "what I want to be when I grow up."

One more self-test item: in the space that follows, explain what you would like to be doing two years after you finish your formal education.

If you found the preceding exercise difficult, you're not alone. All of us seem to know at age six what we want to do when we grow up; by the time we reach the age of twenty, we are clueless. Instead of acquiring cultural information that tells us "how to behave and what everything means," we seem to know less than we did at age six. What happened?

CAREERS: A COMPARATIVE VIEW

In "Career Education from an Anthropologist's Perspective" (Spradley 1973), anthropologist James Spradley observes that in traditional cultures, such as the Amish in northern New York, the Inuit in Central Canada, or the Masai in Kenya, children live close to the world of adult work. As they approach their own adulthood, youths understand clearly what adult work is and what they must do to take it up. There aren't many choices, but there isn't much anxiety, either. The transition is smooth and supported by ritual, such as coming-of-age ceremonies.

The modern West, however, is quite different. Career options are unclear to the beginner. A gulf yawns between young people's lives and what adults do. What kinds of careers are there across that gulf? What do people do in those positions? Young people ask themselves, How do I decide which position is for me? How do I cross this gulf and get into the picture?

Traditional cultures allowed twenty years of adjustment to adult careers. By comparison, Spradley observes, the postindustrial world expects youths to make a more complex transition from sixteen years of schooling to adult work in a matter of months, or as little as a single weekend. And our culture has no ritual to ease the change.

It takes each student a while to assemble some kind of bridge across that gulf between college life and adult life. The national average length of time between graduating with a B.A. and getting hired is six months to one year (James Barrick, personal communication, October 12, 1993). That delay isn't always economically driven—that is, it isn't that there aren't any jobs for liberal arts students. The delay is largely cultural—new graduates simply don't know what to do next. There are too many apparent choices. You don't know how to stand out from the crowd clamoring for that interesting job. You are not even sure what you'd like to do after college (Bestor 1982: 34–35). You have that sinking feeling that decisions made now will seal your fate for years to come.

In anthropological terms, you've not been *enculturated* (meaning, taught your culture) for the task of getting to the next step, of building the bridge between your college life and adult life. As a career counselor at Dartmouth

College puts it, "Although liberal arts majors are qualified for dozens of jobs, they have no idea how to market themselves successfully" (Nadler 1989a: 4).[2]

This workbook operates on the premise that you can become enculturated to the work world while still in college and thus reduce the time after graduation during which you exist as a couch potato in your parents' house. Of course, it is my value judgment that you should want to get on to new things. If you share that value, then you'll need to invest some time to become enculturated, such as by practicing some of the suggestions in this workbook. Doing something now for your career will *in itself* distinguish you from other college graduates as an attractive employment prospect. That is, in my experience, the students who make the effort during their college years to select a starting career track, identify some employers, and prepare themselves for that career are rewarded by finding interesting work more quickly than those who wait until they graduate. As my college's career services officer says, "Looking for a job is itself a job." On-campus recruiters represent only about .005 percent of the nation's employers, so you need to find and woo your employer.

THE TEMPOCENTRISM PROBLEM

Despair not. Even though you don't know much about the careers out there and how to get to them, you're well equipped and well placed to remedy that. Your equipment includes the abilities you've repeatedly exercised in college: handling a number of only slightly related tasks at once, constantly meeting deadlines, and doing research and writing. You are well placed because your university includes experienced anthropology professionals, a career-planning office, libraries, and sophisticated computer search tools.

One problem you still have to overcome is *tempocentrism*. My professor Robert Textor coined this term to describe the inability to think outside of the box of one's current little moment in time. Tempocentrism is like ethnocentrism, which is the tendency to judge other cultures' ways by one's own cultural standards (Textor 1980). Tempocentric thinking views the future as just like the present, only later. Both ethnocentrism and tempocentrism are widespread ways of thinking, in our culture and in others. One of the goals of lib-

---

[2]Nadler's own book, *Liberal Arts Power: What It Is and How to Sell It on Your Résumé* (see Works Cited), offers some excellent guidance in deciding what you want to do for a career, identifying your skills, matching those skills to job requirements, and creating a targeted résumé. Consult his other book, too: *Liberal Arts Jobs: Where They Are and How to Get Them* (1989b).

eral education, however, is to liberate the mind from these self-limiting ways of thinking.

Tempocentric thinking hampers planning, and it's widely recognized that "the idea of planning is still foreign to [students]" (Bestor 1982: 37). That use of the word *foreign* is a nice anthropological way to put the problem. In all likelihood, you haven't had much practice or training in planning beyond a little tactical maneuvering in your course schedule.

Tempocentrism limits career planning in two areas: your vision of yourself and your vision of the world of work. Can you visualize yourself in three years? Can you imagine how much you will have changed? If that is difficult, then consider how much you've changed in the last three years. Quite a bit, I predict, and if you don't think so, ask others who have known you during that time. The usual drawback to tempocentric thinking is that you underestimate how much you'll change to meet new challenges. So you become timid and undersell yourself. Another drawback to tempocentric thinking is that you might jump on today's bandwagon . . . but that bandwagon may not be in the parade in three years.

Breaking out of one's tempocentrism and planning for the future isn't like betting on a horse race. Do not be unduly impressed or intimidated by those "Ten Hottest Jobs in the Next Decade" lists. Such lists are based on the number of positions predicted to open, but they disregard how many applicants there are for each position (Bestor 1982: 36). The trends to take into consideration are the big, systemic ones that are visibly growing now. The American Anthropological Association Web site (*www.aaanet.org*) identifies four such trends that represent opportunities for anthropologists: (1) work is increasingly international; (2) the workforce and market are increasingly culturally diverse; (3) management and decision making in organizations are increasingly participatory; and (4) the flow of communication and information continues to grow.[3] Early in the new millennium, travel and tourism will become the largest industry in the United States (*Faculty Newsbytes,* January 1999). Historical, environmental, and ethnic or religious heritage tours and destinations will need guides, arrangers, writers, and bilingual hosts. Similarly, economist Robert Reich anticipates that the grand forces shaping events in the early twenty-first century will be the contrasting ones of tribalism and information technology (Reich 1999). People will strive for a sense of identity and community (read "culture" here), but they'll do so on cell phones—or wrist computers!

---

[3]If this or any other Web address in this book fails to work, consult my careers Web site for an update: www.potsdam.edu/anth/careers/LatestLinks.

Finally, the U.S. Department of Labor reports an increasingly mobile working population in this country. The average person entering the work-force today will have 3.5 different careers, for ten employers, working about 3.5 years in each position (*Faculty Newsbytes,* January 1998). For many people, the old practice of getting hired once and staying with that job until retirement is gone. A third of today's employed in the United States are "contingency workers" in temporary, part-time, consulting, freelance, or self-employed situations (*Faculty Newsbytes,* September 1999). They're not all languishing in fast-food grills; some people like the mobility and independence. Others convert that insecure job into a more permanent one later. An anthropologist reports, "virtually all of the professionals in my state office began their career at lesser, usually temporary, positions which they used as jumping-off points" (Givens 1986: 15).

The irony is that many of the jobs that anthropology students can prepare for and thrive in involve planning as one of their tasks. So not only do you need to brush up your personal planning skills; you also might consider developing some professional competence in holistic, systemic thinking about the future, as Douglas Raybeck demonstrates in *Looking Down the Road* (2000). Your ability to do both types of planning can be improved while you are in college.

WHAT IS COLLEGE FOR?

Another characteristic of our culture that confuses the career education picture is its faulty grasp of the purpose of a liberal arts education. A recent Yankelovich survey of entering college students, their parents, business executives, and others reveals significant differences among those groups in their understanding of what college is for (Hersh 1997). By definition, if people don't share understandings, then they don't share culture. If you are interested in becoming enculturated to the working world, then consider these survey results.

The study found that many parents and high school students admit that they have little or no idea what a liberal arts education is. They know what they *want* an education to be: a good preparation for that first job. They would prefer specialized training because it makes "practical sense." Business executives don't agree with these views. In general, they are far more positive about the value of a liberal arts education. They are impressed not by the link between college and that first job but by the link to the graduate's entire career life. Executives see the education blossoming in the person over time.

So much for everyone's beliefs and attitudes. Who's actually right? Since the business executives owe their success to finding and directing good

What Liberal Arts Students Can Do to Enhance Their Employment Prospects

1. *Get involved in the career development process early.* During the first two college years, figure out what your talents are, what your interests are, and where they might be further developed and applied. Develop rapport with career counselors and your anthropology professors.

2. *Select minors or elective courses that will demonstrate interest in or be applicable to career objectives.* Leading the list are administration, management, law, finance, technical writing, communications, math and statistics, computers, and public speaking.

3. *Get work experience.* Cooperative education programs, internships, and employment all improve your skills and refine your direction.

4. *Investigate career opportunities.* A survey of seventy-six classics majors found that they were in twenty-five different occupations ranging from business executive to financial planner, from actor to surgeon. Liberal arts students must keep in mind the vast number of occupations for which they are qualified or may become qualified.

5. *Identify your skills, and relate them to the world of work.* Most employers value liberal arts students for their research, writing, speaking, and analytical skills. Together these allow new employees to identify an organization's needs, evaluate information, solve problems creatively, and write clearly and concisely. Learn to speak in terms of a skills vocabulary.

6. *Set specific career and personal goals.* Forget "I want to work with people" or "I want to work in a museum"—these are too vague. Employers want to hear specific and realistic time frames and goals referring to advancement, self-improvement, and accomplishments.

7. *Develop job search and self-marketing skills.* Develop an individualized strategy, and hone your interviewing skills.

8. *Develop realistic expectations.* Expect to start at an entry-level job with little status and a low salary. You'll be on trial and not yet up to full productivity in your new role.

Source: Career Services, SUNY College at Potsdam. Used with permission.

employees, I trust them to have the widest experience and the richest data on this. And those who would hire and enculturate you for many other work settings, such as government, museums, health organizations, and archaeological consulting firms, agree with the business executives.

These survey results suggest that you make two adjustments in your understanding about college and jobs:

1. Your liberal arts education is respected by many potential employers.
2. Your liberal arts education and anthropological training are not as much like a ticket on the first train out of here as they are like your passport and shots—good for the whole journey.

ENLISTING THE TRIBAL ELDERS IN YOUR SPIRIT QUEST

For planning your career, consulting a combination of career counselors and professors works best. I return to career services as a resource in Chapters 4 and 9. As for your professors, they are the elders in the tribe of anthropologists, and you need to learn what they know. They are your guides to the skills and knowledge you'll need to find desirable work, to select a graduate school, or to gain graduate school admission and financial aid.

However, not all professors say much about careers to their advisees or their classes. I know this is so because for years I've advised students from other colleges who have sought me out—when we were at a conference, or when they were home from college, visiting their parents—because these students were suffering from anthro shock that had gone untreated by their own professors.

Why do some professors avoid giving career advice? Some feel they don't understand the work world today, because times have changed since they were looking for work. It is true, after all, that when current college students graduate, many will enter careers that didn't exist twenty years ago. We also know that most people change careers (not just employers, but lines of work) several times in their working life. "How can we know what to advise you today?" some professors ponder. Other professors, finding themselves overworked, consider career advice to be a task someone else should do.

A third and more subtle reason is that some professors think that your concern about how college is going to relate to your occupation is too crass a view of college for them to legitimize by catering to it. In their view, student *vocationalism* (seeing college as a route to a good career) demeans the professor's role from liberator of young minds to gatekeeper to yuppiedom. I have heard professors lament this shift. But in an insightful ethnography of college life, anthropologist Michael Moffatt (1986) led me to reconsider students' attention to jobs. Moffatt suggests that professors who disdain student vocationalism are being hypocritical. After all, professors obtained their career by going to college, and now they carefully manage their own professional career in the college setting, so why shouldn't students want the same? Students expect that their job will place them in the American middle class, where their occupation will be a key element in their identity. They expect that occupation to offer them challenge, growth, rewards, security, and a chance to make the world a better place—all of which sound to me like goals worth supporting as a professor.

In spite of all these reasons why you might not get advice, almost every anthropology department has at least one professor who—because of professional expertise, past work experience, or personal compatibility with you—can offer guidance. Find her or him.

If this chapter has started you thinking about your own career, then I recommend you try Exercise 2, "A Literature Survey," and Exercise 11, "Working with Key Informants" (level 1). These two exercises will guide you in your search for career information.

CHAPTER 3

What Do Anthropologists Do?

In this chapter the term *anthropologist* refers to someone with a master's or doctor's degree in anthropology. To find out what B.A. degree holders are doing, with or without advanced degrees in other fields, turn to Chapter 7.

This chapter serves two purposes: (1) to explode the commonly held idea that anthropologists are all holed up in dark, dusty basements of large universities, and (2) to inspire you to follow in the footsteps of one of the many exemplars presented here.

Each year about four hundred people receive a Ph.D. in anthropology. Another thousand to twelve hundred receive an M.A. in anthropology. About 50 percent of the Ph.D.s are cultural anthropologists, and 30 percent are archaeologists. On average, half of the Ph.D.s are women. These new Ph.D.s constitute less than 1 percent of doctorates in all fields awarded each year (Givens, Evans, and Jablonski 1997).

Today there are altogether twelve thousand people in the United States who have received a Ph.D. in anthropology since the late 1940s (Givens, Evans, and Jablonski 1997). That number will remain constant for the next twenty-five years as the number of professionals dying and retiring matches the number recently graduating (Evans 1997: 17–18). So, there isn't a glut of Ph.D.s now, and there isn't going to be one for a while.

Although it obviously takes talent and time to complete the Ph.D. (see Chapter 6), it is a worthwhile credential—the "terminal degree" in the profession, we say. The person with a Ph.D. is generally given more responsibility and leadership, is usually better compensated, experiences lower unemployment, and has greater mobility between jobs than does the M.A. (*Faculty Newsbytes,* September 1999). In the private sector, however, M.A. recipients are doing nearly as well in the current good economic times.

About 70 percent of recent anthropology Ph.D.s are finding academic positions, and 30 percent are entering government, the private sector, or non-profit organizations (Evans 1997). These proportions have varied over time, depending on the vigor of the economy, the number of students entering college, and the age of the currently employed. Thirty years ago nearly 90 percent of new Ph.D.s went into teaching. Fifteen years ago, less than half did (Baba 1994). Of the majority of new Ph.D.s currently joining faculties at colleges and universities, nearly half are entering departments other than anthropology. They are, for example, in medical schools, academic administration, or special institutes (Baba 1994).

The academic career will be examined first, but I won't dwell on it, because students will have many opportunities to learn about it from their own professors.

EMPLOYMENT IN ACADEMIA

Nearly three-quarters of all anthropologists with Ph.D.s, and some M.A. holders, old and new, are teaching in public schools and institutions of higher learning (David B. Givens, personal communication, January 1995). Even in academia, however, the anthropologist's role is varied. Besides teaching, one may conduct research spending grant money won by competitive application to funding agencies. For instance, I've done fieldwork in the Philippines with funds from the National Institutes of Health (a federal agency) and fieldwork in Newfoundland with support from the American Philosophical Society (a private agency). I've also won a contract from the U.S. Coast Guard to study the impacts of an oil spill.

Another role academic anthropologists adopt is to volunteer professional services within the community, as when some of us from the college helped a nearby town predict the social impacts of a greatly expanded army base. One may earn a fee by signing a consultant's contract with an off-campus group, as my senior seminar and I did when our village recruited us to investigate the role of the Racquette River in village life and history, in preparation for revitalizing the village's riverside attractions.

My father likes to rib me that teaching is a great racket: twelve hours of classes a week and long vacations. In fact, my colleagues and I work about fifty hours a week teaching, advising, supervising student research, and performing many campus "citizenship" duties such as serving on committees, hiring faculty and administrators, attending or organizing workshops, participating in faculty governance, and revising curriculum. Long holidays, including summer, do indeed provide free time—and yes, I take off for a little hiking or snowshoeing during that time. But mostly we use "vacations" for research and writing projects. I'm typing these words during one such winter break.

In 2000, new Ph.D.s employed at colleges like mine were earning on average $37,000 per year, plus fair to good benefits packages with family medical insurance and retirement pension plans (Givens, Evans, and Jablonski 1997). Promotion and salary raises at four-year colleges like mine are based primarily on teaching effectiveness, but within my department we also require each other to remain professionally active. Major research universities place more emphasis on conducting exciting research and submitting articles for major publications. Winning tenure—which means one is no longer subject to periodic fire-me-or-keep-me reviews—comes after about six years of good work. The associate professor promotion usually follows soon after. Perhaps ten years later, promotion to full professor is a possibility. As a full professor, your salary can rise to nearly double what new assistant professors earn. Typically, that's in the $60,000 range in 2000 (Givens, Evans, and Jablonski 1997). That income may be supplemented by teaching summer courses, consulting, and doing contractual work or administrative duties. Many academics, including me, pass over that extra cash for free time to do our research, which earns us little but keeps us vital and flows into our teaching. Creating classroom material, like this book, can earn a modest royalty check.

About every seven years the university allows us to apply for a "sabbatical," or leave with pay for a semester or two to pursue further professional development. My colleagues and I use that time for original research and writing, reading, or further formal education. We pay for this research by winning grant competitions from our university, government, and private foundations.

In spite of all the attention this chapter devotes to nonacademic anthropology, because that is the kind most people are unfamiliar with, an academic career is an excellent one, and I recommend it. Your advisors may tell you that there aren't any academic jobs, but they're fifteen years behind the times. Clearly, there is competition: right now there are only 63 percent as many university positions open as there are new Ph.D.s to fill them (Evans 1997). Still, you have only to be in the top half of applicants to be a serious contender. Some of those academic jobs are temporary or part-time, but so are many nonacademic positions you might enter. Finally, a large cohort of baby boomers, including me, is going to retire in the next ten years. Just when you're finishing your Ph.D.! See Exercise 4, "Demography," for evidence of this. In my own department, for example, in 2000, four out of eight teachers were hired in the last three years, and three more are going to be needed to replace retirements by 2010.

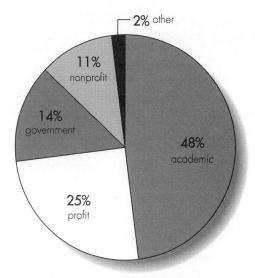

FIGURE 3.1   NAPA Members' Work Settings.
Data from Johnson 1991.

EMPLOYMENT OUTSIDE ACADEMIA

Since the mid-1980s nonacademic employment has evolved from being a fall-back for those who couldn't get a teaching job to being a highly desirable way to practice anthropology. The pathbreakers in government, industry, consulting firms, and nonprofit organizations have done much to convince the nonacademic working world that anthropology is valuable. And they've made your task to follow them easier.

By the mid-1980s, 30 percent of recent Ph.D.s were taking nonacademic positions, and 63 percent of those positions were closely related to the graduates' training (Baba 1994: 177). Ninety-two percent of the job seekers were employed within two years of earning their doctorates (Fillmore 1989). As a group, these nonacademic anthropologists are paid more than academics are paid, and they report greater satisfaction with intellectual stimulation and job security (Givens, Evans, and Jablonski 1997: 319).

What are these nonacademics doing? Anthropologists who work full-time or part-time outside academia have their own branch in our professional association called the National Association of Practicing Anthropologists (NAPA). In a 1990 survey of its members, NAPA found that 52 percent were employed primarily outside academia. Figure 3.1 shows where they were working. The 2 percent in the "other" category were employed by international organizations such as Cooperative for American Relief Everywhere (CARE) and the World Health Organization (Johnson 1991: v; Baba 1994).

Salaries of nonacademic anthropologists vary greatly, depending on the type of employer, geographical location, and the anthropologist's degree, skills, and prior experience. Some directors of research in the private sector make over $100,000 (Singer 1994: 7). Entry-level workers with a B.A. and no experience who enter a rural human services program may start at $20,000 per year, and Ph.D.s at $30,000. M.A. holders without experience entering government or community organizations start at perhaps $29,000, and Ph.D.s at $35,000. Anthropologists with some experience move into corporate or medical settings for $5,000 more. By midcareer, anthropology Ph.D.s are earning anywhere between $42,000 and $95,000, with good benefits packages. Their job titles typically are "program manager," "research fellow," "education director," or "public relations director" (Givens, Evans, and Jablonski 1997: 312).

Here are examples of M.A.s and Ph.D.s using their anthropology across a wide range of work settings. Some of these practitioners (as we call those who aren't primarily professors) I have met, and some I have corresponded with. Others have been described in the press. Nearly every issue of the journal *Practicing Anthropology* and the newsletter *Anthropology News* has one or more profiles of anthropologists doing interesting work. Other examples can be found in books such as *Applying Anthropology* (Podolevsky and Brown 1999), *To Make Our Work Useful* (van Willigen, Rylko-Bauer, and McElroy 1989), and *Anthropological Praxis* (Wulff and Fiske 1987).

Deciphering and Translating

In my own research and consulting in the private sector, I have discovered full-time anthropological practitioners in roles that range from research scientist in a corporation-based artificial intelligence laboratory, to trainer in the cross-cultural communications industry, to international marketing executive in a pharmaceutical firm, to president (and founder) of a consumer research consulting firm. In many of these roles, anthropologists were deciphering and translating for their sponsors the behavior of cultural "others," including "others" in the form of employee occupational groups, customers, and foreign nationals.

Marietta Baba, Director of the Business and Industrial Anthropology Program, Wayne State University, Detroit, Michigan

Source: Baba 1994: 179.

Practicing Cultural Anthropologists

Cultural anthropologists have been employed in the federal government since before World War II, but now state and local governments also hire them in large numbers.

- Fred Bloom is a research anthropologist in the Behavioral Research Intervention Branch of the Center for Disease Control. He studies behaviors that spread sexually transmitted diseases (Barone 1999).

- Nora Dudwick studies poverty in Eastern Europe and Russia for the World Bank. She conducts ethnographies of local problems and cultural practices so she can assist engineers and economists to establish effective development projects using bank funds (Kuehnast 1999: 32).

- Thirteen contract ethnographers make up the Applied Ethnography Program of the National Park Service, in the U.S. Department of Interior. These Ph.D.s team up with archaeologists to study historic and prehistoric landscapes or structures needing federal protection as educational or sacred sites.

- Other U.S. government agencies in which anthropologists work are Housing and Urban Development, Bureau of Indian Affairs, National Science Foundation, General Accounting Office, National Oceanic and Atmospheric Administration, National Cancer Institute, Health Resources and Services Administration, Agency for International Development, the Smithsonian Institution, National Institutes of Health, and the Peace Corps (Singer 1994: 9).

Anthropologists with Influence

By my estimates, there are hundreds of anthropologists working within governmental agencies (Environmental Protection Agency, National Park Service, National Forest Service, Bureau of Land Management, etc.) and just over a thousand anthropologists working in the U.S. on U.S.-based environmental problems. In terms of impact, [this] paid and voluntary interaction with local, state and international NGOs [nongovernmental organizations] may represent the area with the greatest capacity for influencing people's lives and futures.

Barbara Rose Johnston, Director of the Society for Applied Anthropology's Environmental Anthropology Project and Senior Research Fellow, Center for Political Ecology

Posted on EANTH-L listserv Feb. 4, 2000, and published with permission.

- M.A.s and Ph.D.s also hold state and local government posts such as director of planning and development in Arizona, program specialist for a county alcohol rehabilitation school in California, research associate for the New Jersey Farm Bureau, regional supervisor for Alaska's Department of Fish and Game, legislative assistant in Wisconsin, and equal opportunity coordinator for the Department of Education in Wyoming (Givens 1986: 1).

Corporations have also been seeking and hiring cultural anthropologists (see the box titled "Management Discovers Cultural Anthropology"). Xerox, Nissan, and General Motors are among the growing number of businesses that employ anthropologists to study them ethnographically, to analyze their corporate culture, and to improve staff morale, task efficiency, and service to customers.

- Paul Hilton, M.A. in cultural anthropology from New York University, has become the new co-manager of Dreyfus Corporation's Third Century Fund, a mutual fund that invests only in socially and environmental benign business securities. Hilton's career to date has been devoted to responsible investing and consumer behavior (Dreyfus Semiannual Report, November 1998).
- Citicorp hired Steve Barnett, Ph.D., as a vice president for research. Barnett developed a research design to provide warning signs when credit card holders were so in debt that they might default (Jones 1999).
- Suzanne Gibbs began as a consultant to Bigstep.com, conducting studies of what small businesses need in Web services and how people with mouse in hand actually use the Internet. Now she's a full-time member of the company's User Experience Team (Greengrass 1999a: 34).
- The Young and Rubicam advertising agency hired anthropologists to do participant observation with mail carriers in the U.S. Postal Service. The agency sought ideas for promoting the service's functions. Ethnographers found that the public has a good attitude toward the mail carriers, seeing them as trustworthy faces humanizing a large bureaucracy. So Young and Rubicam's ads for the Postal Service emphasized the image of the neighborhood postal carrier (Foltz 1989).

Large corporations may offer big projects and big salaries, but more than half of Americans work for employers with one hundred or fewer employees (U.S. Bureau of Census, reported in *Faculty Newsbytes,* Spring 2000). Anthropologists also work in small private consulting firms.

Management Discovers Cultural Anthropology

Cultural anthropologists inform managers that different people from different backgrounds and cultures will have to be integrated into organizations. To avoid forfeiting economic growth and power to the Japanese, South Koreans, Germans, French, and others, U.S. managers must scientifically study the human resources available for employment, training, and education. Cultural anthropologists have a wealth of knowledge, insight, and recommendations that managers need to use more and more in the 1990s.

. . . Cultural anthropology has made significant contributions regarding the effect of culture on organizations. In the future, as firms expand their activities overseas, anthropology undoubtedly will also provide managers with valuable insights as they attempt to perform the functions of planning, organizing, and controlling in different cultural environments.

Source: Donnelly, Gibson, and Ivancevich 1992.

- Cathleen Crain (M.A., McMaster University) and Niel Tashima (Ph.D., Northwestern University) founded LTG Associates in 1982 in California and expanded to Washington, D.C., in 1984. LTG's work has focused on improving access to health care for ethnic minorities and vulnerable populations. The firm has worked on projects involving HIV/AIDS, aging, hepatitis, substance abuse, tuberculosis, child abuse and neglect, and food security. LTG is now providing monitoring, evaluation, facilitation, and research services to international health programs. Clients include the U.S. Agency for International Development. More information about LTG Associates can be found at their Web site (*www.ltgassociates.com*).

- Robbie and Belinda Blinkoff, cultural anthropologists, have formed Context-Based Research Group, Inc., with Chuck Donofrio, CEO for Richardson, Myers, and Donofrio, a marketing and communications firm in Baltimore, Maryland. Recent projects include two global studies for Procter & Gamble, usability testing for LeapFrog Toys, and e-commerce research with Sapient. Context also directs its own longitudinal project on youth and technology called GenWired 2000 in thirty-five homes across the United States. More information can be found at their Web site (*www.contextresearch.com*). The group recruits ethnographers through its Web site (*www.anthrojob.com*).

- Gordon Bronitsky is president of Bronitsky and Associates, with offices in Denver and Bergamo, Italy. Gordon began as an archaeology Ph.D.

with a specialty in ceramics but found greater prospects promoting
Native American artists to overseas audiences. In the last few years he's
guided a Comanche flute player on a tour through Ireland, a Pueblo
hot glass artist through Finland, and a group of Chinle Valley singers
through Italy (Bronitsky 1999).

A growing number of anthropologists are employed in nonprofit organizations, a label that covers everything from museums and charitable or community development organizations to political, cultural, and environmental
advocacy groups. Here are a few examples.

- Jonnie Marks is the director of research at a large urban treatment
  agency for abused or challenged children. She conducts research, coordinates with other agencies, writes grant proposals for agency support,
  and conducts training sessions for employees (Barone 1999: 37).
- Steven Schwartzman is a member of the core staff of the Environmental
  Defense Fund (EDF) in Washington, D.C. As one responsible for EDF's
  international program, Schwartzman "creates strategies to protect tropi-
  cal rainforests and their indigenous peoples, particularly the native
  peoples of the Brazilian rainforests. [He] promotes the adoption of
  environmentally sound lending policies by the World Bank, other
  multilateral development banks, and national governments"
  (*www.edf.org/aboutEDF*).
- Sheila Dauer holds a Ph.D. in anthropology from the University of
  Pennsylvania and is on the staff of Amnesty International, U.S. Section
  (AIUSA), where she directs the Women's Human Rights Program. She
  creates strategies and mobilizes AIUSA staff, volunteer leaders, and
  membership to take action on behalf of women around the world who
  are imprisoned, tortured, "disappeared," unfairly tried, or threatened
  with death for their beliefs, their peaceful activism, their gender, or their

Politics and Baby Food

These days, a graduating anthropologist is likely to be analyzing policy for
a Detroit city councilman, studying infant-feeding trends for a pharmaceutical company that produces baby formula, or . . . making sense of social and
cultural trends for movie executives or soap manufacturers.

Source: Heller 1988.

connections with men who are sought by the authorities. AIUSA has been advocating U.S. ratification of the U.N. Women's Convention (CEDAW, the Convention to Eliminate All Forms of Discrimination Against Women). Currently the women's program is campaigning for laws in six U.S. states to protect women in prisons and jails from rape and other sexual misconduct by correctional officials. (See the AIUSA Web site at *www.amnestyusa.org/women.*)

Practicing Archaeologists

Archaeologists saw vast opportunities open up beyond the university when Congress passed the National Environmental Protection Act (NEPA) in 1970. This legislation mandated that any alteration of the landscape that uses federal funds must first conduct an environmental impact assessment, including assessing the impacts on historical and prehistoric resources. Alterations include the erection of roads, dams, and buildings and digging or filling the land. States have passed similar laws, such as New York's State Environmental Quality Review Act, for projects involving state funding.

This enterprise, known as cultural resource management (CRM), has offered great employment opportunities. The volume of assessment work became so great that archaeologists established private firms with full-time staffs of field directors and grant and report writers. Federal and state agencies also hired more archaeologists.

CRM work and compensation varies according to one's experience and leadership responsibilities. Fieldworkers, who are often B.A. holders with some undergraduate field school experience, earn between $9 and $13 per hour digging and as much as $17 per hour in lab work (Boyd 1998). The work is driven by contracts, so jobs are temporary, highly seasonal in northern latitudes, and sometimes require living in a motel or a tent. A per diem allowance covers living expenses, but pay rarely includes fringe benefits, and on rainy days, canceled digs mean no wages. Nevertheless, work is plentiful these days. Companies around urban areas always need good crews. An electronic discussion list devoted to announcing and reviewing these opportunities is *www.onelist.com/subscribe/shovelbums.*

I was impressed to learn that my department recently had five alumni working in CRM for the New York State Museum in Albany. They were all B.A. students. Four had been anthropology majors, and the other was a history major who had attended our archaeology field school.

Field crew chiefs in CRM projects or firms are more experienced than the shovel workers and often have M.A.s. They earn between $11 and $16 per hour. Field directors are usually full-time staff members of the firm and are given oversight of the entire contract. The position requires an M.A., as well as writing and organizational skills, but earns between $13 and $17 per hour plus benefits. The anthropology Ph.D.s who run the firm, win the contracts, and write the reports earn between $18 and $30 per hour. For more information on CRM, see the Web site *www.cr.nps.gov.*

The federal government alone employs nearly a thousand professional archaeologists in five departments and the Tennessee Valley Authority. The Army Corps of Engineers, for example, has 159 archaeologists on staff, and the Department of Agriculture has 399, mostly in the Forest Service and the Soil Conservation Service. These public agency archaeologists seek potentially valuable sites, inventory them, and protect them from disruption during construction (or at least collect information before the site is destroyed). They also research and develop some sites for appreciation by the public and produce educational materials showing how the site reveals the past and how pot hunting destroys history.

While some archaeologists are protecting ancient Native American sites, historical archaeologists focus on the remnants of the more recent past to fill out documented history. They delve into the ruins of the pioneer, colonist, farmer, tenement dweller, factory worker, and slave in the last five hundred years. The "Careers in Historical Archaeology" Web site reports that an M.A. in historical archaeology, representing about two years' work, is necessary and often sufficient (*www.sha.org/sha_cbro.htm*). In 1995, historical archaeologists in state and local agencies started at salaries ranging from $18,000 to $30,000 per year. Those in universities or federal agencies, which require a Ph.D., started with salaries from $25,000 to $40,000 per year.

Historical archaeologists work both on land, to document an old bottle factory, for example, and underwater, to salvage sunken vessels or inundated villages. Their research is done to comply with state and federal laws and to mitigate the impact of development such as tourism or parking lots. Historical archaeologists spend much time forming recovery plans and protection policies with historians, museums, students, labs, land planners, developers, legislators, and community preservation groups.

- Varna Boyd is an archaeologist and partner in Greenhorne and O'Mara, Inc., based in Washington, D.C. While in graduate school in historical archaeology, Varna joined a cultural resource management project that the Pennsylvania Department of Transportation was undertaking in order to improve a section of highway. She began as crew chief and, as the project mushroomed, rose in the organization to become a partner. In a five-mile stretch of road, the project found sixty-eight archaeological sites. During the four and a half years of work, Varna's company hired hundreds of fieldworkers and handled a $5 million budget (Boyd 1998).

- David West Reynolds began as a classical archaeologist and ended up in Hollywood. While conducting an archaeological survey in Egypt searching for Roman roads, he trekked off to Tunisia for a break, to photograph and walk the locations where *Star Wars* scenes were filmed. His fandom turned into a consultancy when LucasFilms learned of his knowledge. The film company engaged him to help create *Star Wars: Episode 1—The Phantom Menace.* He stayed on to write books for them, reconstructing whole imaginary societies out of the fragmentary scenes that the films presented (Greengrass 1999b).

- Valerie Talmage earned a master's in anthropology, specializing in archaeology, and won a position as a staff archaeologist on the Massachusetts Historical Commission. Nine years later, Talmage is executive director of that commission and has been appointed the state's historic preservation officer. Her archaeology background helps her understand the sociocultural setting of a historical property, and working on digs has improved her organizational skills. Talmage acquires state and federal grants and manages a multimillion-dollar budget.

- Frank McManamon also began in the Massachusetts State Historic Preservation Office with an M.A. in archaeology. From the state office he moved on to become the northeast regional archaeologist for the National Park Service and earned his Ph.D. writing about the sites he studied on the job. He moved again to become chief archaeologist in the Park Service headquarters in Washington, D.C., writing policy for a staff of nearly four hundred and advising the entire Department of the Interior on archaeological matters. Recently, Frank headed the team of experts analyzing the controversial Kennewick Man discovery before final resolution of the disposition of the remains.

Practicing Biological Anthropologists

Most biological anthropologists teach and do research at universities and colleges, in departments of anthropology, anatomy, physiology, nutrition, genetics, physical education, biology, geology, paleontology, prehistory, psychology, human biology, zoology, and in interdepartmental social science programs (American Association of Physical Anthropologists, n.d.). More than 15 percent of academic biological anthropologists are based in medical schools, where they teach in departments of anatomy, pathology, and medical genetics (Wienker 1991: 28). Some teach in high schools. About 25 percent of biological anthropologists are employed outside of the university for at least part of the time. Some work for various state and federal government agencies, such as state health departments; the Smithsonian Institution; the National Institutes of Health and Aging; the U.S. Army Research, Development and Engineering Center; and the U.S. Army Central Identification Laboratory (Wienker 1991: 29; see also Corner and Gordon 1996).

Other biological anthropologists are staff members of zoos and zoological research institutes such as the Oregon and New England Regional Primate Centers. Some natural history museums, forensic labs, and law enforcement agencies have physical anthropologists on salary or on contract. Physical anthropologists have been hired by the American Red Cross and animal welfare groups. Still other professionals are in the private sector, meaning that they work for commercial labs such as Ross and Battelle Laboratories, consulting firms, or large corporations that conduct their own product research and design. The following short profiles suggest the range of possibilities.

The opportunities for employment in biological anthropology vary by specialty. Anthropologists who work on health-related issues are numerous, whereas forensic anthropologists, for example, are rare. There are only about 150 professional forensic anthropologists in the United States, and only fifteen are doing such work full-time (Neely 1998: 159). Undergraduate anthropology majors love forensics, but they'll have to combine that with other specialties like genetics, criminology, or disaster research in order to increase their chances of using their forensics professionally.

- William C. Rodriguez III is a forensic anthropologist with the Armed Forces Institute of Pathology. Forensic experts often work with archaeologists to reconstruct crime and disaster scenes and to identify human remains (Overbey 1999). Rodriguez was a member of an FBI team that traveled to Kosovo at the request of the World Court in September 1999 to exhume mass graves for evidence of war crimes.

- Jeff Long investigates the genetic and environmental underpinnings of complex diseases as a senior investigator at the National Institutes of Health, which is part of the United States Department of Health and Human Services. He is a member of a team studying the genetics of alcoholism in a variety of populations including Europeans and Native Americans. The team proposes no simple one-to-one relationship between one's risk for complex disease and one's genes or environments, but genetic results have been interesting. A graduate student working in his research section recently demonstrated that a locus linked to the Y chromosome may contribute to differences among men at risk for alcoholism.

- Jerry Snyder runs a Tucson company, Biodynamics International, which sells research in biomechanics (what's going on when the hand removes a jar lid by twisting, for example) and accident trauma (how being rear-ended in a car produces whiplash, for example). The company has five times as many contract offers as it can accept (Wienker 1991: 28).

- John McConville's company, Anthropology Research Project, Inc. (ARP), of Yellow Springs, Ohio, has been in business for fifty years. ARP conducts applied anthropometry, which involves collecting measurements of the human form to determine the best sizes and shapes for clothing and equipment. In government contracts, ARP answers questions like these: Where should the dials be located so that nuclear power plant operators can best keep track of events? How should military or power line repair equipment be modified so that women can use them? (Wienker 1993: 21).

- F. John Meaney is chief of Genetic Diseases for Indiana's State Board of Health. He oversees the entire state's genetic evaluation and counseling services. He also teaches workshops to medical personnel and concerned parents (Meaney 1995). His statistical and research skills permit him to conduct sophisticated analyses of large databases and still pay careful attention to individual variation within the population. Meaney acquired key skills through postdoctoral study in medical genetics; his recommendations for preparation for this career have been published in the *American Journal of Physical Anthropology* (see Ward and Meaney 1995).

Practicing Linguists

Language plays a role in every human activity, so it's not surprising that linguistics, the study of language, has found application in a wide variety of fields, from law and medicine to advertising, translation, and education. Linguistic methods and scholarship have provided testimony for the conviction of murderers and have protected the *Mc* in *McDonald's* from trademark infringement. Linguists have developed effective speech therapies for victims of stroke and have studied the way teachers and students talk to each other to improve teaching. Linguists have explained why there is little hope that we can write software to prevent children's finding Internet pornography simply by blocking certain key words from search engines.

Linguists are translators (of written text) and interpreters (of the spoken word), but they also work as encryptors and speechwriters. Text analysts unpack the meanings in crucial documents, such as communiqués between warring parties, to discover what is really being admitted or demanded. Linguists have assisted tribal peoples in developing an orthography (a standardized written form) of previously unwritten languages. Linguists have helped lawmakers to prepare (or oppose) legislation dealing with language in multicultural America. They teach languages and accents to actors, missionaries, and role-playing museum guides.

Here are a few examples of linguists at work outside the university. I found some of these in an interesting collection by Dallin Oakes (1998).

- Barbara Joans, a linguistic anthropologist at Idaho State University, was hired as an expert witness in the defense of six Bannock Shoshone women accused of defrauding the Social Security Administration. Joans successfully demonstrated by linguistic testing that the women were not sufficiently fluent in English to understand government agents when the rules were explained. The case against the women was dismissed, and subsequent Social Security contacts with the Shoshone utilized an interpreter (Wulff and Fiske 1987).

- Bob Cohen of Lexicon Naming assists companies to create successful product names by paying attention to the symbolism of the phonemes— the meaningful sounds—in names. He conducts survey research among speakers to learn which sounds connote speed, comfort, and dependability. He has found, for example, that stops (*b, p, d*) connote dependability better than fricatives (*v, f, z, s*). Thus a *Bazia* auto sounds more dependable to English speakers than does a *Vazia* (Cohen 1995).

- Deborah Tannen has earned a national reputation examining how miscommunication occurs because of linguistic differences between men and women. Through participant observation, focus groups, and questionnaires in several corporations, Tannen has learned that in their communication with colleagues, men and women speak or write differently when they promote their accomplishments, suggest changes, give orders, or criticize. These ways of talking were learned in girl groups and boy groups while growing up, but the girl-group style is at a disadvantage in the corporation. Tannen brings these findings to the attention of managers so that both styles will be correctly interpreted (Tannen 1995).

- Steven Cushing was funded by the Aviation Safety Reporting System, a research group for the National Aeronautics and Space Administration, to study the communication errors that contribute to aircraft accidents. He found that ambiguous expressions in the lingo that grew ad hoc in the profession as technology advanced led to misunderstandings and ultimately to tragic accidents. Now the Safety Reporting System issues regular warnings on language threats to safety. The use of technology to screen and clarify communication between pilots and control towers, for example, is being tested (Cushing 1993).

- Marc Okrand, a linguist of Native American languages, was hired by the producers of *Star Trek III* to create realistic dialogue for the Klingons, inhabitants of one of the more famous Star Trek planets. Okrand went on to create a complete language and a dictionary of Klingon, which have become cult classics. He continues to do artificial language work in the film industry (Okrand 1998).

IN-DEPTH PROFILES

The following three career histories illustrate how one gets from the B.A. to interesting professional work. All three professionals are working outside the university. They represent three of the four subfields of anthropology. I selected them because they are colleagues or former students whose work I admire. Their biographies are very different, but these people were all well educated and flexible (more than they thought!), they developed their networks, and they had drive. They also saw how to connect to some rising trends in America's agenda, particularly medical and environmental issues. You can conduct a similar study of an individual whose career you admire by performing Exercise 7, "Life History: A Recent Ph.D."

> "Still Working on Those Statistics!"
> —*Peg Weeks, cultural anthropologist*

Peg earned a B.A. in cultural anthropology at SUNY Potsdam and entered graduate school at the University of Connecticut. In Connecticut she studied with an advisor who maintained extensive connections in China, so Peg lived and taught in China for two years. Her doctoral dissertation was on the changing status of Chinese women in the post-Mao period. Nine years had passed since her B.A., which is the norm for Ph.D. students.

Ph.D. in hand, Peg began applying for teaching positions in the Connecticut and Rhode Island region. She managed to find temporary positions for a course here and there for a couple of years, but the gypsy life of the unsettled academic was discouraging. Married and raising children, she didn't want to pull up roots for teaching jobs in Florida or Utah, so she decided to look nearby for project administration and applied research positions.

Like all beginners, Peg ran up against the "experience" requirement for these positions, so she wasn't making the final cut. Her first break came when she was hired for a year at the University of Connecticut as an assistant coordinator of a women's studies project. This opened the door to a year as acting director of the university's Center for Educational Innovation office. These positions gave her enough of those vaunted experience chips to reenter the competition for other administrative positions.

Peg spotted an ad in her city's newspaper for a position at the Institute for Community Research (ICR) in Hartford, seeking a research director to lead a study of AIDS among injection drug users. The position called for quantitative and medical experience, but Peg persevered, insisting that she could pick these up on the job. She was hired, and eleven years later, she has become the associate director for research and one of the seven full-time professional anthropologists on the staff. She oversees projects funded by grants and contracts from the National Institutes of Health to explore the health risks to women, drug users, African Americans, Puerto Ricans, and others. Peg's task, she reports,

> is to hold the collaboration of community and research groups together, which takes social skills, and to promote understanding of each other's mission among agencies, which takes communication skills. Constantly I try to move the AIDS research agenda beyond the usual quantitative and psychological approach to include an ethnographic approach. We might, for example, accompany drug users through their day to see what they actually do that puts them at risk of infection. I also write grant proposals, hire and supervise fieldworkers, train interns . . . and I'm still working to master those statistical and quantitative methods! (Peg Weeks, personal communication, March 6, 2000)

Peg's advice to readers is to get training in quantitative methods, even if you hope to nudge your employer toward using qualitative methods such as ethnography. The lesson I draw from her biography is that one mustn't take the published job description too literally, as a barrier, but see it as an area for negotiation. Peg convinced the ICR that she was worth hiring even if she didn't meet some of their criteria. For more practice interpreting published position vacancies, perform Exercise 14, "Interpreting the Text."

"I Never Imagined I'd Be Doing This"
—Deborah Cox, archaeologist

Deborah completed her B.A. in education and history at Rhode Island College, but participation in archaeological digs during college prompted her to minor in archaeology also. By the time she graduated, she knew she didn't want to be a teacher, so she went to work for the Public Archaeology Lab (PAL) at Brown University, across town from her college. The lab had been growing rapidly because Rhode Island was funding many highway construction projects, all needing environmental and archaeological assessments. Deborah's experience in college was a winning meal ticket, and she was much in demand for field crews.

She completed an M.A. in archaeology while based at Brown, and she assumed more responsibilities in the organization. Eventually, university support for PAL was cut, so staffers established themselves as the new PAL, an independent nonprofit firm. The company presented itself, as it says in its promotional literature, as "addressing the needs of the diverse constituencies involved in large, complex projects requiring environmental review, preservation planning, and archaeological or architectural surveys."

PAL recently received a National Transportation Design Award from the U.S. Department of Transportation for preserving the site of a railroad roundhouse built in the 1880s in Whitman, Massachusetts. PAL created an archaeological park, combining historic preservation with public education. The roundhouse park enhances its neighbor, the train station for the newly restored Old Colony Line.

As PAL president, Deborah's work is to win contracts, manage a staff of forty full-time and fifteen temporary employees, and conduct public education programs about CRM. She also brokers good relations among the many parties to a large project (such as neighborhood associations, state agencies, academics, and so on) and manages the business of the company.

"I never imagined I'd be doing anything like this when I graduated," Deborah reflects. Her advanced degree sharpened her skills to "think clearly, learn quickly, and communicate effectively." She's had to pick up some M.B.A.-type business knowledge on the job. Because she was busy in an interesting, dynamic position and did not plan to teach, Deborah did not return to school for a Ph.D. For archaeologists who'd like to emulate her, she recommends that they acquire some understanding of business, improve their quantitative skills, and gain fieldwork experience early in their career.

"Is Your Line in the Water?"
—*Marilyn London, biological anthropologist*

Marilyn graduated with a B.A. in anthropology from George Washington University, whose professors introduced her to projects and staff at the Smithsonian Institution, which proved to be a valuable network connection later in her career. She entered the biological anthropology program at the University of New Mexico and finished her M.A. degree in two years. She continued to take courses for the Ph.D., specializing in skeletal biology. She worked as a graduate teaching assistant for a few years and was a founding editor of a journal to publish student research. "I always loved reading and writing," she says, and she has put this love to work throughout her career.

Marilyn's life as a freelance consultant began in New Mexico. She worked on forensic cases and a mass disaster for the State Office of Medical Examiners, supervised a paleontology field school, analyzed skeletal remains for the Zuni Pueblo's own archaeology project, worked with the state archaeology lab to document recently discovered Civil War casualties, and served as a museum aide at Chaco Canyon National Monument.

After freelancing in New Mexico for eight years, but before completing the Ph.D., Marilyn moved to Rhode Island so her husband could attend graduate school at Brown University. While in New England, she worked with the university and local hospitals and taught short courses through area continuing education programs. One hospital project involved analyzing nurse interventions to reduce women's cardiac deaths. Another project had her surveying parents and videotaping parent/child interactions to understand the development of infant temperament. At Rhode Island Hospital, she maintained a database on twelve hundred patients and served as epidemiologist and biostatistician for the renal division. As in New Mexico, she took on forensic projects for the state medical examiner's office, for whom she is still the forensic anthropology consultant.

Six years later Marilyn was back in the Washington, D.C., swirl because her husband had received a postdoctoral appointment at the National Institutes of Health. She renewed the contacts she had made when earning her B.A. there. She took every opportunity to acquire more teaching experience, lecturing in forensics and osteology for the Smithsonian, the National Museum of Health and Medicine, a high school of science and technology, adult education programs, and the University of Maryland. Her experience in journalism led to contracts editing technical manuscripts, Web pages, and publications for universities, the National Cancer Institute, and the Smithsonian.

The capital area teems with short-term consultancies. Marilyn performed skeletal analysis for the Smithsonian and for engineering firms doing CRM. In one project, she analyzed the remains of a cemetery uncovered in New York City during the renovation of City Hall Park. She expanded her network by accepting volunteer executive duties for Washington area anthropological and scientific associations and editing their journals. When a colleague from the Smithsonian took a position at the Virginia Museum of Natural History, she hired Marilyn to assist in producing an Ice Age exhibit and catalog. Marilyn also joined the Atlantic Regional Disaster Response Team, funded by the U.S. Department of Health and Human Services. As if this wasn't variety enough,

Marilyn coauthored an anatomy lab kit sold as an educational toy at the Smithsonian and is now helping to develop a companion skeleton kit.

Marilyn's career to date reveals the power of networking, of putting oneself in the way of breaking opportunities. Although teaching jobs were scarce when she was leaving graduate school, she found many chances to teach at good schools. Although forensic work for anthropologists is even scarcer, she found that work, too. Employment opportunities can be serendipitous (lucky accident), Marilyn says, but you make your own luck. "Is your line in the water?" And whether she is working in hospitals or designing Web pages or educational toys, she has maintained her anthropological perspective—the biocultural, holistic, comparative angle on human behavior and biology. More advice from Marilyn may be found in her chapter, "Contracting as a Biological Anthropologist," in Alan Ryan's *A Guide to Careers in Physical Anthropology* (2000).

Well suited to the themes of this chapter are Exercise 3, "Participant Observation: Part 1," Exercise 8, "Internetworking," and Exercise 10, "Organizational Analysis."

CHAPTER 4

How Do I Find Out Whether Anthropology Is for Me?

The two elements of a good career choice are knowing about the position and knowing about yourself. Both elements are improved by efforts you can make now. You can learn about the position through Exercises 7, 11, and 13. You can learn about yourself through Exercises 5, 12, and 15. Below are six activities that you can pursue to help you decide whether you really have enough interest in and talent for a career that depends upon anthropology.

1. **Test yourself.** Your college's career services office, like mine at Potsdam College, maintains a battery of tests that help you articulate your strengths and preferences. Some tests are fairly high-tech, like SIGI+, a computer-operated career-matching system. You can experiment with the Keirsey Temperament and Character inventory on the Web (*keirsey.com*). The Princeton Birkman Quiz (*www.review.com/birkman/*) is a similar inventory. There are also good tests on paper, like the Myers-Briggs Type Indicator, the Strong-Campbell Interest Inventory, and a number of values clarification exercises.

The main value of such tests is that they give you the opportunity to take a thorough and fresh look at yourself with an expanded, more precise vocabulary. "I like to work with people," for example, is quite vague, but under scrutiny it may turn out to mean something more specific and useful, such as

- "I like to broker among different groups," or
- "I like small teams dedicated to one project," or
- "I like to delegate and supervise," or
- "I like to help the helpless."

Most career services offices also produce a workbook with some self-discovery exercises. The office at Potsdam has one called *Selecting Your Career Lab Book*. When you have compiled some data on yourself and careers, make an appointment with the career counselor to intepret the data and define some next steps.

2. **Take courses.** Explore not only the four subdisciplines but also the different approaches of several instructors. Only then can you know where your particular anthropological calling lies. (I decided eventually that I missed my calling as a physical anthropologist. When I was an undergraduate twenty-five years ago, I switched to anthropology from premed, still deeply interested in anatomy, microbiology, and disease. But my university didn't offer much in physical anthropology, so I became a cultural anthropologist.) To sharpen your discovery process, visit some of the professors in their offices and ask them to describe one of their courses or show you their labs. Talk to some of their more advanced majors and research assistants.

3. **Compare yourself** to those who have entered the profession. Why did they become anthropologists? What personality traits, talents, ambitions, and forms of intelligence combine to make a dedicated anthropologist? Hortense Powdermaker, in her classic *Stranger and Friend* (1966), observed that for her and other anthropologists she knew, having some life experience that marginalizes you, so that you view even your own native culture from a slight remove, is the common experience. Powdermaker was a "red diaper baby"—the child of radical labor organizers. I was an "Air Force brat"—the child of parents who moved often. Some books address this topic of how one decides to become an anthropologist. One example is *Others Viewing Others: The Ethnographic Career* (Fowler and Hardesty 1994). *Anthropology and the Peace Corps* (Schwimmer and Warren 1993) also discusses why people become anthropologists.

4. **Do some anthropology outside the classroom.** Get a summer job in fieldwork, lab work, data analysis, or museum work. Should you not find an appropriate summer job, then do volunteer work for a while. Ask to help professors conduct research. Apply for internships and volunteer opportunities. Attend a summer school program with a strong active component. A summer school archaeology dig in northern New Mexico is what convinced me that anthropology was fascinating. For a brief and efficient introduction, conduct the shadowing part of Exercise 3, "Participant Observation."

5. **Read books** focusing on the anthropologist's work. Some recent ones are *Bones: A Forensic Detective's Casebook* by physical anthropologists Douglas Ubelaker and Henry Scammell (1992), *Dancing Skeletons* by ethnographer Katherine Dettwyler (1994), or *First Fieldwork* by Barbara Gallatin Anderson (1992). The reader *Applying Anthropology,* edited by Aaron Podolevsky and Peter Brown (1999), has many examples from all four subfields. For applications of cultural anthropology, I recommend Robert Wulff

Anthropology Careers Web Sites

Cultural Anthropology or All Fields

AnthroTech Virtual Library	*vlib.anthrotech.com/job_opportunities*
American Anthropological Association	*www.aaanet.org/carplc.htm*
Metropolitan State College, Denver	*clem.mscd.edu/~career/majorin.html*
Northern Kentucky University	*www.nku.edu/~anthro/careers.html*
National Park Service	*www.ncptt.nps.gov*
National Association of Applied Anthropologists	*www.oakland.edu/~dow/napafaq.htm*
University of California at Berkeley	*ls.berkeley.edu/dept/anth/handbook .html*

Archaeology

Society for American Archaeology	*www.saa.org*
Archaeological Institute of America	*www.archaeological.org*
University of Montana	*www.taylor.anthro.umt.edu /jobs/default.htm*
Illinois State Museum	*www.museum.state.il.us/ismdepts /anthro/dlcfaq/html*
Society for Historical Archaeology	*www.sha.org/sha_crbro.htm*

Biological

American Association of Physical Anthropologists	*www.physanth.org/careers/*
University of California at San Diego	*www.weber.ucsd.edu/~jmoore/ bioanthro/brochure1.html*
	www.weber.ucsd.edu/~jmoore/ bioanthro/brochure2.html
University of North Carolina at Wilmington	*www.uncwil.edu/people/albertm/ faqs.htm*

Linguistics

Rutgers University	*www.equinox.rutgers.edu/info/faq/ career_opps.html*
University of Iowa	*www.uiowa.edu/~linguist/ ug-after-grad.html*
Stanford University	*www-linguistics.stanford.edu/ cgiw-bin/linguistics/undergraduate/ whydeclare.pl*

and Shirley Fiske's *Anthropological Praxis* (1987) or Van Willigen, Rylko-Bauer, and McElroy's *Making Our Research Useful* (1989). For archaeology, see Ivor Noel Hume's *Martin's Hundred* (1982). Also, try Exercise 2, "A Literature Survey." What archaeologists are doing in the world and how they feel about their careers are thoroughly covered in Melinda Zeder's *The American Archaeologist: A Profile* (1997).

A student interested in the private sector will realize what anthropology can do by reading Peg Neuhauser's *Tribal Warfare in Organizations* (1990) and *Corporate Legends and Lore* (1993). Students interested in law and legislation must read Jack Weatherford's *Tribes on the Hill* (1985), about an anthropologist as insider with the U.S. Congress. *Mainstreaming Anthropology* (Hanson et al. 1988) has profiles of professional anthropologists working in prisons; in the social service departments of city governments helping the elderly, poor, and children; and in state government working to renew an urban neighborhood. *Anthropology for Tomorrow* (Trotter 1988) contains Elizabeth Briody's report of interviews with eight professionals working in business, government, and consulting firms.

Anthropological consulting is a growing field, as is evident in Chapter 3. *Anthropology and Management Consulting* (Giovannini and Rosansky 1990) explains the field, and *Research and Consulting as a Business* (Davis, McConochie, and Stevensen 1987) offers four profiles of professional anthropologists who are consultants, owning or employed in firms with names like Cultural Dynamics, Inc., and Corporate Research International. Another good overview of how anthropologists work in the private sector is Marietta Baba's *Business and Industrial Anthropology* (1986). Baba discusses anthropologists in consumer behavior research, product design, internal organizational analysis, intercultural training for employees, and international business management.

A number of periodicals can also provide insight. Someone curious about cultural resource management, public archaeology, or government work should read *Common Ground,* published quarterly by the U.S. National Park Service's Archaeology and Ethnography Program. Another on that topic is *CRM Monthly,* published by the Park Service's cultural resource office (see Works Cited for ordering information). The monthly newsletter of American Association of Museums is *Aviso,* and members of the American Public Health Association read the newsletter *The Nation's Health*.

Useful Web sites are popping up like mushrooms (but sometimes liquefying just as fast). The box titled "Anthropology Careers Web Sites" describes examples of anthropology sites that include sections on career options.

6. **Talk with a professional anthropologist** using Exercise 11, "Working with Key Informants."

. . . And They're Off!

The B.S. versus the B.A. in the Race for a Good Job

The B.S. takes an early lead . . .   The B.A. is weaker than the B.S. at career entry. Because the B.A. doesn't show much commitment to a specific career, it is not clear what job training is still needed or whether the employee will stay with the job.

It's neck and neck on the backstretch . . .   Once under way in a career track, responsibility on the job increases and the B.A.'s organizational, communication, and problem-solving skills, among other widely applicable abilities, become more important.

And the B.A. wins, pulling away! . . .   In several corporate longitudinal studies of employees, the B.A. student often became the supervisor of the B.S. student. The flexibility of the B.A. is especially helpful in adapting to career changes: four such changes during one's working years is now the norm.

WHICH SHOULD I CHOOSE FIRST: THE CAREER OR THE MAJOR?

If you have no idea about which career you're interested in, then choose your major from among the subjects you enjoy the most and get the best grades in. There *is* a connection between that major and your career interest—you just don't know what it is yet. There is no perfect connection between an anthropology major—or *any* liberal arts major—and a specific career.

Here's proof: Lawrence and Anita Malnig, authors of the bestselling career guide *What Can I Do with a Major In . . . ?* (1984), found in their nationwide surveys that managers and administrators came from eighteen majors; medical doctors from twelve different majors; law, computer programming, advertising, and hospital management each drew graduates from ten different majors (Conniff 1986: 48). Lawrence Malnig says that "students look at a far too limited range of careers" (Conniff 1986: 49). Malnig's advice to liberal arts students is to know yourself:

- Evaluate what you've learned.
- Identify the aptitudes you've discovered and developed.
- Then look for careers that match your knowledge and aptitudes.

To conduct such a self-study, investigate some of the resources mentioned in this chapter and try Exercise 15, "Know Thyself," and Exercise 5, "The Résumé."

Other research, conducted in the corporate world, shows that compared to the more specialized B.S. holder, the B.A. holder is at a disadvantage in finding that first job, but the advantage reverses in time (see the box titled ". . . And They're Off!").

CHAPTER 5

What Knowledge and Abilities Will I Need?

MARKETABLE SKILLS

The term *marketable skills* is a misnomer. There are few skills that a liberal arts student acquires that *aren't* marketable. But there are trends and fashions, not only in which skills are considered hot this year but also in what vocabulary is used to describe those skills. As an anthropologist, you're equipped to identify the fashions and adapt to them by rephrasing what you're good at.

Here are some skills that anthropology majors have the chance to develop in my college. Many of these are available where you study, too.

- Interacting with people of diverse cultures, making allowances for differences in customs and beliefs
- Providing insight into social problems by supplying information as to how problems, such as those that result from aging, conflict, or bereavement, are dealt with in other cultures
- Interviewing people to obtain information about their attitudes, knowledge, and behavior
- Using statistics and computers to analyze data
- Adapting approaches used in public relations, marketing, or politics to different population groups
- Working cooperatively with others, adapting to varied sociocultural conditions
- Appraising, classifying, and cataloging rare, old, or valuable objects
- Designing and lighting attractive displays
- Repairing, reconstructing, and preserving cultural artifacts by selecting chemical treatment, temperature, humidity, and storage methods

- Drawing maps and constructing scale models
- Photographing sites, objects, people, and events
- Interpreting or translating
- Using scientific equipment and measuring devices
- Analyzing craft techniques
- Demonstrating ethnic arts learned through participant observation

The following twelve abilities are often acquired through the anthropology major. Treat the following as a checklist of abilities you will find useful in your future work, so that you will want to acquire them and then highlight them when presenting yourself to potential employers.

1. Social agility	In an unfamiliar social or career-related setting, you learn to quickly size up the rules of the game. You can become accepted more quickly than you could without this anthropological skill.
2. Observation	You must often learn about a culture from within it, so you learn how to interview and observe as a participant.
3. Analysis and planning	You learn how to find patterns in the behavior of a cultural group. This awareness of patterns allows you to generalize about the group's behavior and predict what they might do in a given situation.
4. Social sensitivity	Although other people's ways of doing things may be different from your own, you learn the importance of events and conditions that have contributed to this difference. You also recognize that other cultures view your ways as strange. You learn the value of behaving toward others with appropriate preparation, care, and understanding.
5. Accuracy in interpreting behavior	You become familiar with the range of behavior in different cultures. You

	learn how to look at cultural causes of behavior before assigning causes yourself.
6. Ability to appropriately challenge conclusions	You learn that analyses of human behavior are open to challenge. You learn how to use new knowledge to test past conclusions.
7. Insightful interpretation of information	You learn how to use data collected by others, reorganizing or interpreting the data to reach original conclusions.
8. Simplification of information	Because anthropology is conducted among publics as well as about them, you learn how to simplify technical information for communication to nontechnical people.
9. Contextualization	Although attention to details is a trait of anthropology, you learn that any given detail might not be as important as its context and can even be misleading when the context is ignored.
10. Problem solving	Because you often function within a cultural group or act on culturally sensitive issues, you learn to approach problems with care. Before acting, you identify the problem, set your goals, decide on the actions you will take, and calculate possible effects on other people.
11. Persuasive writing	Anthropologists strive to represent the behavior of one group to another group and continually need to engage in interpretation. You learn the value of bringing someone else to share—or at least understand—your view through written argument.
12. Assumption of a social perspective	You learn how to perceive the acts of individuals and local groups as both shaping and being shaped by larger sociocultural systems. This perception enables you to "act locally and think globally."

Source: Office of Career Services, SUNY Potsdam. Used with permission.

Marketable Experiences Available in the Anthropology Major

Working with a team, such as an ethnographic or archaeological research project

Supervising a work team of peers

Policy making based on social science research data, problem-solving methods, and professional ethical standards

Designing research projects and applying for grants

Producing a research paper in anthropological format and style

Orally presenting research results

Using a variety of ethnographic data-collection techniques: ethno-semantics, proxemics, life histories, ethnohistory, folklore, event analysis, genealogies, and so on

Technically producing and editing a scholarly journal

Showing leadership in a preprofessional organization, such as a student anthropology society or honors society

Developing or enhancing public relations for a museum

Designing, building, installing, and acting as docent for museum exhibits

Coaching, instructing, tutoring, and team teaching with peers

Studying a second language

Adjusting to new behavior patterns while immersed in another culture

---

According to Lawrence and Anita Malnig, authors of *What Can I Do with a Major In . . . ?* (1984), the recommendation is simple:

> Students who master just these three skills in *any* major have "as sure-fire a ticket to success as it's possible to buy": the ability to learn fast in a new situation and to do it on one's own; ability to analyze, evaluate, and interpret data; ability to communicate effectively in speech and writing. (Conniff 1986: 52)

I concur, except that I can identify additional transferable skills learned in the anthropology major that might be useful in certain situations. The box above is part of a list that I give to SUNY Potsdam anthropology majors.

Again, the point of these lists is to identify skills that anthropology offers and to label training and experience in a language that has meaning for others.

When surveyed by the periodical *Job Outlook,* employers in both the private and public sectors replied that they wanted better communicators, more young applicants with some hands-on experience, and better career guidance (*Faculty Newsbytes,* September 1998). Improvements in all these areas are possible during your college years.

Job interviews have become increasingly sophisticated among big employers. A large northeastern private hospital that hires many kinds of applicants, including social scientists, engaged a consulting firm to develop an interview procedure for identifying the best applicants. What that employer wants reveals much about what you need to develop. The interview probes up to seventeen areas of competence; for several of these areas, anthropology students can be well prepared. Areas include "client-orientation," "interpersonal communication," "team management," "conceptual thinking," "analytical thinking," and "tolerance for ambiguity." Your challenge is to identify opportunities to practice these skills before graduating.

When groups of practicing anthropologists (meaning those not primarily teaching) are convened and asked to advise students following in their footsteps, the responses are strikingly consistent from one group to another. My experience chairing such panels matches what graduate students heard at a recent conference (Guerron-Montero 1998: 7–8):

- Even in graduate school *pursue interdisciplinary study.* The challenges of the real world are not divided up neatly like academic departments and courses.

- Practice *teamwork* and acquire experience *administrating* something.

- Learn to design and carry out a *research project* and to write *grant applications* to fund it.

- Develop your *methods tool kit* to conduct a variety of qualitative and quantitative analyses.

Archaeologists in particular urge students to develop management skills so they can organize projects and supervise staff to act quickly on an interesting site before it's lost to vandals or bulldozers (Givens 1996: 1).

ANALYZING THE FIT BETWEEN THE JOB AND YOU

Our professional association, the American Anthropological Association (AAA), has produced a nonacademic job manual for Ph.D.s, *Getting a Job Outside the*

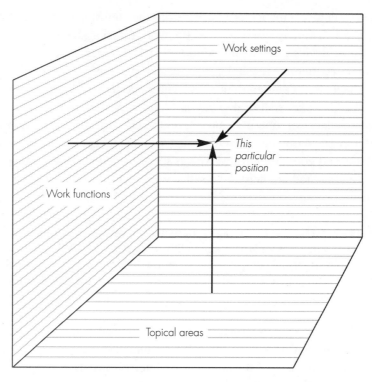

FIGURE 5.1   The Nonacademic World of Work. *Source:* Adapted from American Anthropological Association 1982.

Academy (American Anthropological Association 1982). The manual offers some good advice about reconceiving your training and experience as fitting into the job market, and I will pass on some of that advice here.

According to the manual, trained anthropologists don't have to abandon their anthropology and retrain to enter nonacademic work. Finding employment is a matter of matching one's skills to the employer's needs. The manual advises readers, as I have done here, to study their potential employers so as to make that match seem obvious.

To establish the right match, think of the nonacademic world of work as arranged in three dimensions, within which you decide where to position yourself. The three dimensions are (1) topical areas, (2) work functions, and (3) work settings (see Figure 5.1).

Topical areas are the substantive fields of study, such as kinship, rural development, or medical anthropology. Because your training is very broad, your ability to bridge the gulf that sometimes separates specialists in social sciences, history, biology, or the plastic arts will be attractive. However, topical area is less important in nonacademic positions than academics think.

The most valuable capabilities you have are the "transferable" ones that can be applied in a variety of contexts to the work functions.

Work functions refer to the kinds of activities performed. Work functions most commonly needed are research, planning, administration and management, and communications. Specific research skills that anthropologists acquire, like statistical analysis, cartography, computerized bibliographic searches, or questionnaire development, are attractive. Communications, too, seem obvious, encompassing writing and presenting, publishing, promoting, and good listening, as well as sophisticated linguistic competence. As for planning and administrative skills, we develop and rely on those a lot more than we think we do.

> In many ways, the fieldwork experience gives anthropologists a significant "comparative advantage" with respect to the skills it demands in administration, interpersonal communication, network development, and logistical planning. (American Anthropological Association 1982: 7)

Work settings refer to the types of organizations where you work: local, state, or federal government, nonprofit or commercial research, international service organizations like the Agency for International Development (AID) or CARE, private voluntary organizations like the National Trust for Historic Preservation, or corporations like Microsoft and Ben and Jerry's. Each of these types of work settings has a different "corporate culture" and avenues for entry, which the AAA manual (and the works in its bibliography) describes.

Further discussion of this "corporate culture" idea and how liberal arts graduates thrive there may be found in Michael Useem's *Liberal Education and the Corporation: The Hiring and Advancement of College Graduates* (1989). Useem's conclusions are based on a large survey research of 532 corporations and 505 middle and senior managers. Case studies of liberal arts graduates in "corporate culture" are included.

The box titled "What Anthropology Students Need" lists two examples of work functions and work settings that anthropology B.A.'s might be interested in.

ADVICE FROM ALUMNI

Again, let the data speak. In a survey we conducted of over six hundred alumni from thirty-two anthropology B.A. programs in the northeastern U.S. (Kratts and Hunter 1986), one of the questions we asked was, "Knowing what

What Anthropology Students Need

Position Title	Work Requirements	Work Setting
Supervisor, historic sites, cultural resource management	Graduate degree in archaeology or history; helpful: courses in public administration, communications	Historical societies; U.S. Department of the Interior; some state park services; city landmark preservation commissions
Public relations representative	Courses in public relations, journalism, communications, or courses in a field related to the firm's business, such as biology or finance	Mostly large corporations, public relations consulting firms, manufacturers, public utilities, transportation, insurance companies, trade or professional associations, museums, educational institutions, health and human service organizations, government

Source: Levy 1991.

you know now, would you major in anthropology again?" Eighty-two percent of the respondents said yes. In addition to checking boxes on the questionnaire, many jotted remarks after the questions. A child-support enforcement officer wrote,

> Realize that in anthropology you will
> a. never be wealthy
> b. need a sense of humor
> c. find a healthy respect and love for the emic[4] approach
> d. take a great deal of satisfaction in your work

While remaining loyal to the anthropological perspective, most alumni had specific advice about what to study besides anthropology. They urged anthropology students to take courses outside of their major and to acquire some hands-on experience. The courses recommended for study were usually math, science, computing, communications, statistics, and economics.

---

[4]"Emic" refers to studying what the informants of the studied culture find meaningful; it is contrasted with "etic" or studying what the outsider with a cross-cultural perspective finds interesting.

Although most alumni recommended subjects to study, an undercurrent of opinion suggested that more basic personal qualities were perhaps more important. An alumnus who is now a staffing consultant wrote, "Your education serves [just] as a backdrop. It's perseverance, ambition, and character that will get you the job that you're after."

EXPERIENCE IS INVALUABLE

The second piece of advice the alumni gave was to acquire some hands-on experience beyond listening to lectures and taking tests. The experience may be divided into four types: (1) research, (2) employment, (3) internships, and (4) volunteer work.

Research opportunities may arise as part of a course, as a solo effort or a team project. Our department offers a few courses that guide students in collecting original oral history and material culture data in our town, analyzing the data, and presenting reports. We also have an archaeology summer field school that teaches site survey, excavation, and lab work. Finally, we have a museology course that teaches students to research and design museum exhibits. Students may also conduct research by assisting a professor in his or her work. Our college awards some small grants specifically for professor-student research teams. I've won three or four of these and have watched my student partners grow more self-directing, more creative, more . . . *employable.*

Employment opportunities refer to both summer jobs and part-time work while going to school, as well as full-fledged cooperative education arrangements wherein the student takes leave from school and works full-time. Several of my advisees have discovered interesting careers by working part-time for various offices on campus, such as alumni affairs, continuing education, and food service. In these posts they became acquainted with professional people other than their professors, practiced administrative and communications skills, managed subordinates, learned more about computers, discovered how their anthropology is useful, and in general strengthened their confidence and ambition. Departments like ours also hire students during the year as research assistants, helping professors conduct bibliographic searches, analyze or catalog data, edit manuscripts, and so forth. Some student assistants are hired to help in introductory physical anthropology labs, where they also learn fossil casting and other procedures.

Internships are the third category of practical experience. More than two-thirds of employers that emphasize college hiring like to "test drive" their job candidates through internships before offering permanent employment (*Faculty Newsbytes,* Spring 2000). Internship pay is low or nil, but the intern

Some Anthropology Internship Web Sites

U.S. National Park Service	*www.cr.nps.gov*
U.S. Agency for International Development	*www.usaid.gov/about/employment/ intern.htm*
NAPA Mentor Program	*www.policycenter.com/policycenter/ intern/intern.htm*
Environmental Anthropology Internship	*www.sfaa.net/eap/abouteap.html*
American Public Health Organization	*http://web.sph.emory.edu/phemploy.nsf/ by+job+type*
Congressional Research Service	*http://lcweb.loc.gov/crsinfo*
World Bank	*http://wbln0018.worldbank.org/hrs/ hrs_www.nsf*
Washington Association of Practicing Anthropologists	*www.smcm.edu/wapa/gen-an.html*
Society for Applied Anthropology	*www.telepath.com/sfaa/eap/ abouteap.html*
Smithsonian Institution	*www.si.edu/resource/faq/start.htm*
Student Conservation Association	*http://216.32.56.72/vol/vol.htm*
Federal agencies (social science)	*www.usajobs.opm.gov/ei13.htm*
General internships listings	*www.internships.com*
	www.snybuf.edu/~cdc/ internship-links.html
	www.goshen.edu/soan/soan961/htm

often gets an overview of the enterprise and is assigned interesting tasks. In recent years I have helped students arrange internships in a history museum, a nursing home, a sheriff's department, and our village food pantry. I also placed interns with the county environment management council and Big Brother–Big Sister, Inc. In most cases we arranged that the internship be credit bearing and culminate with a final report reviewing what the intern did, what was learned, and how anthropology was used on the job.

There are also good internship opportunities for undergraduates or recent B.A.s with Cultural Survival, Inc., the Natural Resources Defense Council, the Smithsonian Institution, and state government offices, to name just a few. It is possible to convince an organization that interests you that it *should* have an intern, even if it hasn't had one yet, and that the intern should be *you*.

Many of the organizations mentioned in Chapter 3 as hiring anthropologists also offer internships, usually for master's and doctoral students. Some

---

Using the Ethnographic Approach Is a "Marketable Skill"

Whereas other social sciences moved toward *quantitative* methods of
research (testing theory by using survey questionnaires and repetitive
observations), anthropologists most often conducted *qualitative* research.
Called "the ethnographic approach," this method yields a highly detailed
account of the culture of a particular group. Its primary purpose is the
discovery of what is really going on, not the testing of theory. . . . It is
this qualitative approach that has turned out to be most valuable in the
world of business and industry.

Source: McCurdy and Carlson 1984: 235.

---

of the largest are the National Park Service, InterAmerican Foundation, Peace
Corps, Centers for Disease Control, U.S. Agency for International Devel-
opment, CARE, Habitat for Humanity, the World Bank, and the National
Institutes of Health. Visit their Web sites for more information. The box titled
"Some Anthropology Internship Web Sites" lists a few that I've explored.

Volunteer work is nearly the same thing as an internship but without the
glorified label. The nice thing about volunteer work is that you can get your
foot in the door of an organization you would really like to work for if you
are willing to start for nothing. The sacrifice shows your commitment to the
organization, builds your connections and job experience, and often gives
you the competitive edge over other applicants when a position does open
up. If you have to hold down a paying job, then volunteer on the side.

I encourage my advisees to volunteer for local positions in which they
will develop appropriate skills or meet the right people. In my department,
two of those positions are the Student Anthropology Society executive committee and the *Collegiate Anthropologist* journal editorial staff. It pays to volunteer for such groups: a couple of years ago one of my students got her
first-choice job teaching in a Native American school precisely because she
had experience editing and publishing our department journal, which was a
model for the newsletter the school wished to begin.

To develop the themes of this chapter, try Exercise 5, "Transcultural Self-
Presentation."

CHAPTER 6

After the B.A.

Graduate School?

As their senior year begins, anthropology students need to decide whether they want to go to graduate school the next year. At SUNY Potsdam, a few of them decide affirmatively and begin the process of requesting catalogs and applications and scheduling the Graduate Record Exam (GRE).

Meanwhile, most anthropology students—even those I think will profit from graduate school—decide to stop school for a while and get a job. Why? They say they are tired of studying and they have large debts to pay. No doubt this is true. I also think they lack the confidence or the direction to go on immediately. After a year or two in the working world, however, they discover that entry-level work is fairly dull and underpaid, that they are more talented than many of their coworkers, and that they are ambitious after all, so their interest in jump-starting their career by going back to school is rekindled. As a matter of fact, many do resume their education within a couple of years of earning the B.A., studying everything from chiropractic to elementary school education, anthropology, and environmental management. And they do well.

This pattern of delay by my students used to bother me, but now I accept it. Conversations with colleagues across the country have convinced me that this is a widespread pattern.

So, should *you* go to graduate school right after getting your B.A.? Here's the test: If you can answer yes to all of these questions, then of course you should go now.

_____ Am I persistent?

_____ Am I self-motivating and self-directing?

_____ Am I willing to work hard?

_____ Am I good at reading and writing?

_____ Do I know what I want to study?

_____ Do I know what I might do with the degree?

A no on any of those questions is probably enough to disqualify you—for now, anyway. Shouldn't I have included a question above about having the money? As I show later in this chapter, money is not that big a problem. Shouldn't I have included a question above about being brilliant? Brilliance is like perfect pitch: sometimes it's helpful, sometimes it's merely a freakish talent, but it's not necessary (and it certainly isn't sufficient!) for success in life or in graduate school.

WHAT'S IT LIKE? AN ETHNOGRAPHY OF GRAD SCHOOL

Generalizing about every kind of program, from veterinary medicine to archaeology, is pointless. Although some of what I say in this chapter is pertinent to all graduate training, I prefer to confine my remarks to graduate school for anthropology, which is still very broad because in the United States alone there are over ninety programs. If you are thinking about graduate school in another academic discipline, like history or French, then much of the following also applies to you. Law school, medical school, and other professional schools have their own peculiarities (and their own guidebooks).

Here's what my departmental colleagues and I say each fall semester at our graduate school advice panel for undergraduate majors.

A Different Culture

First, graduate school is as different from college as college was from high school. Graduate school is very focused. You'll spend most of your time in the department, lab, or library, in the company of other anthropology graduate students. In college, you could succeed if you passed the right courses, whether or not you were well known to any professor; in graduate school, by contrast, your success depends in part on picking the right professor to be your patron. He or she will help you find grants, jobs, and research opportunities. Without her or him, you're adrift, and if you haven't found your patron after a year and a half, you're going to have trouble getting a degree.

In graduate school there is a ratcheting up of the expectations and the work compared to what you did in college. In high school, the teacher told you what to do for next class; in college, the professor gave you a schedule and you kept track of what to do. In graduate school, the professor will suggest books and expect you to teach yourself kinship, population dynamics, or semiotics. In college, a C grade was accepted for the major. In graduate school, anything less than a B+ is not good enough.

Second, graduate school is not a waiting game; it's the fast lane. Don't go to graduate school because you don't know what to do with your life. Graduate study requires far too much commitment to be a good place to kill time.

Third, picking the right graduate school is a research project at least as large—and certainly more important—than any you've done in your anthropology major so far. After all, you took only four or five years to get a B.A., but it will take longer than that to get a Ph.D. Getting into the graduate program that is right for you is an achievement demanding effort and time. If you're willing to work hard at that, you probably are ready to work hard in graduate school. And since you've honed your anthropological skills, you can and should use them to pick the school and get accepted.

The Master's Degree

The first year is mostly a matter of proving yourself in basic theory and area courses: archaeology, cultural anthropology, linguistics, and physical anthropology. Usually your graduate professors will want to teach you anthropology all over again, fast forward; after all, some of your classmates were not anthropology majors. You will probably also begin preparing for a set of comprehensive exams in theory, or on a subfield or geographic region, or you will prepare to submit a master's thesis, to be done at the end of the second or third year. You will spend some summer time in field or lab work or special training programs.

The Doctorate

You will finish the M.A. in two or three years, at which point it will have become clear that you do or don't want to work toward a doctorate with someone on the faculty there. If you continue, you'll probably combine a teaching assistantship with a wide mix of elective classes and grant writing for your doctoral research. You will assemble a doctoral examination committee of professors, mostly within the department, but usually including an external examiner from another department. Your patron serves as the committee chair.

Doctoral research varies by subfield. The physical anthropologist may stay on campus the entire time or may travel to watch primates, collect blood samples, or measure fossil casts. The archaeologist goes to a dig for anywhere from a few months at a time to a year, returning periodically to analyze the data. The linguist and ethnographer usually go into the field for an extended period; the average is about a year. The field, however, might be a primary care clinic on the other side of town. As the survey of recent Ph.D.s described in Chapter 3 reveals, many doctoral researchers fund their own work, but others win government grants or piggyback on their patron's grants.

You write your dissertation while you are teaching part-time or are otherwise employed, or while you are still receiving grant funds. Your committee reads and comments on drafts, asking for changes. The oral defense is usually low-key—you know at that point that they're probably accepting it. We survivors like to joke that your best strategy in the oral is to provoke an argument among committee members and then get out of the way and let them tire each other out. Finally, submit a couple of very neat copies of the dissertation to the university, and you're done!

These days, students take from eight to ten years from starting the M.A. to finishing the Ph.D. The average age at completion is thirty-five years. This may shock you, but remember that many of these students entered graduate school after working for a while, or they didn't study full-time. The average time to complete the anthropology Ph.D. is about one year longer than for most social science Ph.D.s, partly because of the time spent in fieldwork (Evans 1997).

SHOULD I GO FOR THE MASTER'S OR THE DOCTORAL DEGREE?

Graduate programs come in three types, each with its strengths and drawbacks.

Type 1   Programs that offer only the master's degree.

William and Mary's historic archaeology M.A. is an example. The faculty in these programs pay more attention to their new graduate students than most Ph.D. programs do, but if you change your mind and decide to pursue a doctorate, you must apply to another institution and start over again to build a reputation and win patrons. If you intend to put some working years between your M.A. and your (possible) Ph.D., these schools deserve a close look.

Type 2   Programs that offer a Ph.D. but also award a master's degree as a legitimate terminal degree.

The University of Florida's Interdisciplinary Program in Anthropology is an example. M.A.s are offered that focus on agriculture, medicine and nursing, and urban planning, to name just a few. This type of program offers maximum flexibility for you to change your mind about your goals while in training. However, the faculty may be a little schizoid about whether it

Go Interdisciplinary

Take your anthropology B.A. into master's programs like the following. This list is incomplete and neglects the west coast, but it illustrates the range of options.

Documentary film   Temple University
Human genetics   Pennsylvania State University
Linguistics   Indiana University
Information science   University of Michigan
Tourism   Rochester Institute of Technology
Journalism   Columbia University
Ethnomusicology   Wesleyan University
Criminology   Northeastern University

Thanks to Ellen Kintz of SUNY Geneseo for sharing this information.

is producing research doctorates or applied master's. The mix is tricky, and the results vary from institution to institution. If the professors are dedicated to applications in their own professional work, as many are at the University of Florida, then the combination is compatible.

Type 3   Programs that primarily offer a Ph.D. but provide the master's as a consolation to those who do not go on.

The University of Michigan, my alma mater, provides an example. The M.A. is usually a general anthropology degree, without the focus you'll find in Type 2 programs. On the other hand, many of the most prestigious graduate schools in the country are of this type. Those who drop out of the Ph.D. program can proudly display the big-school M.A. on their résumé.

EXAMPLES OF SPECIAL GRADUATE TRAINING

Here are just a few examples of special graduate programs that emphasize anthropology. They are chosen haphazardly from my files and represent my subjective list of interesting programs. This list illustrates the range of possibilities; it does not tell you where you should go.

George Washington University, in Washington, D.C., offers an M.A. emphasizing development anthropology. Given the proximity to the federal government and international agencies, students easily find internships and positions with the U.S. Agency for International Development, the State Department, the World Bank, or nonprofit organizations such as Africa Crossroads, which is a nongovernmental Peace Corps.

The University of Georgia, in Athens, Georgia, has been shaping a very strong environmental studies emphasis in recent years by hiring new faculty and designing new courses. Cultural and physical anthropology and archaeology courses are all involved.

Wayne State University in Detroit offers M.A. and Ph.D. degrees in business anthropology through its Business and Industrial Anthropology Program.

The University of Kentucky, in Lexington, has a long-standing reputation for its master's program with an applied emphasis. Kentucky places students in internships so that by the time they complete the degree, they have experience and sometimes a job waiting with the people they interned for.

The University of Massachusetts at Amherst produces a strong cadre of historical archaeologists at the M.A. and Ph.D. levels. I've seen their students make presentations at conferences. The College of William and Mary, in Williamsburg, Virginia, is also known for its historical archaeology. For both schools, their home states are deeply committed to recovering and preserving their rich histories, so graduates often find work with the state.

The State University of New York (SUNY) at Buffalo has a field-based master's training program, called Research Careers in Anthropology. Students accepted into this program are fully supported through the degree but, even more important, are more likely than at other schools to conduct field research as master's students. SUNY Buffalo is a Type 3 school in my typology, which means it expects the talented students to continue through the Ph.D.

Columbia University has one of the oldest and most prestigious historic preservation graduate programs in the country. The Program in Early American Culture, a collaboration between the Winterthur Museum and the University of Delaware, provides a multidisciplinary M.A. or Ph.D in the study of material culture with special emphasis on decorative arts and household furnishings. The Graduate Program in History Museum Studies, at the Cooperstown Museum in central New York State, offers a two-year M.A. in museum administration, curatorial duties, and exhibitions.

As early as 1982, there were seventeen institutions in the country offering M.A.-level training in cultural resource management (CRM; Bush 1981: 4). In my region, the State University of New York at Binghamton and the University of Connecticut are active in this field. More are identified below.

The University of South Florida (USF) has one of the longest-standing applied anthropology programs, specializing in urban and medical anthropology and public archaeology. Its applied medical M.A. or Ph.D. requires an internship, but the department has arranged for many opportunities in the

Tampa area. It has tracked its M.A. graduates and learned that most enter the public sector (government and not-for-profit organizations). More of its Ph.D. graduates enter the private (for-profit) sector (Fiske and Chambers 1996).

Memphis State University's applied program is also long-standing and, like that of USF, specializes in urban, medical, and archaeological studies. Its urban anthropology master's degree leads to positions in city planning, education, housing, and community revitalization. The department runs its own social service organization, the Center for Voluntary Action Research.

Another veteran in applied anthropology is the University of Maryland. Its interdisciplinary M.A. is modeled after the Master's in Business Administration (M.B.A.) degree, emphasizing the skills needed to run an organization. Students are required to minor in another discipline and to complete a three-semester internship. The university is conveniently located close to federal opportunities for internships and jobs in Washington, D.C.

PLANNING FOR GRADUATE SCHOOL

Once you decide to pursue graduate education, in anthropology or a related field, you construct a plan—a schedule of decisions and tasks. Your university and the manuals described below offer more thorough guidelines for this kind of planning. Here's a short sketch of a typical calendar.

Eighteen to twelve months before you intend to enroll, you should be a whirlwind of preparation.

❏ You've selected a small group of institutions that match your academic goals. Ideally, you have visited some of these institutions or at least conducted research about them (see the box titled "What to Look for in a Graduate Program").

❏ You've registered for the Graduate Record Examination (GRE).

❏ You've searched for national scholarships for which you might be eligible.

Between twelve and nine months before, the paperwork increases.

❏ You are preparing for the GRE, drafting your personal essay, and collecting admission and financial support applications from your short list of preferred programs.

❏ You select people you would like to have write recommendations for you.

By eight months before enrollment, you've submitted all your application materials.

❏ You've checked to make sure your complete application was received.

Five months before enrollment, when you learn the results, you make a selection and notify all programs that have accepted you.

❏ You notify those people who helped you.

HOW TO SELECT A GRADUATE PROGRAM

Students Jennifer Ramirez, Pamela Hanlon, and Loni Wallace developed these ideas in our senior seminar for anthropology majors. After helping to research this section, they took their own advice: Jennifer went to graduate school in public health, Pam in the ministry, and Loni in archaeology.

Using *Peterson's Guide*

The most detailed directory of graduate programs, including those for anthropology but for many other fields as well, is *Peterson's Guide to Graduate and Professional Programs* (Peterson's staff 1999). Begin with the "Directory of Graduate and Professional Programs by Field" in the front of volume 1, and use the "Index of Directories and Subject Areas" in volumes 2–6 to locate the volume for your field of interest. For example, anthropology and archaeology are in volume 2, beginning on page 1392. Institutions are briefly profiled in volume 1, and their programs are described in greater detail in volumes 2–6.

In this guide, each program description is submitted by the institution itself, which is standard for education guides, so you can't assume the description is an impartial evaluation. Information typically includes address, level of program, the number of faculty, the number of students (part- and full-time, and by gender), the number of minority students, the average age of students, the percentage of applications which are accepted, degree requirements, entrance requirements, cost, financial aid, faculty research interests, research budget (how successful the faculty has been at winning grants), phone number, and whom to contact for an application. Some program descriptions include even more information.

Using the AAA Guide

The best publication for selecting a graduate program in anthropology is the American Anthropological Association's *Guide to Departments of Anthropology*. Published annually, the guide contains a wealth of relevant information for anyone interested in a career or graduate study in the field of anthropology. Your anthropology department office usually has a recent copy of the guide that you can look at, as do some professors in the department. Or, if you like, you can purchase the most recent copy of the guide from the AAA (see the Works Cited section of this workbook).

The guide contains a name index of anthropologists in postsecondary education and research institutions, statistics about recent degrees, dissertation topics, and a couple of other short summary sections. The most elaborate and useful section of the guide is entitled "Departments." In this section, anthropology departments are listed alphabetically by institution. Community colleges, museums, research institutions, and government agencies that employ anthropologists are also listed in this section. Each institution's listing includes information about faculty and their research interests, number of majors, special programs, anthropologists in other departments, degree requirements, and the number of degrees granted.

There are several ways to use the information included in these entries. For example, if you can name a particular institution where you might like to study, you can check your areas of interest against those of the faculty in the anthropology department there to see how well your interests match. Or, if you are interested in pursuing a degree outside of anthropology, you might want to see whether any anthropologists are on the faculty of the program you are interested in. My student Jennifer (mentioned at the beginning of this section) chose to study public health at the University of South Florida in large part because several medical anthropologists there also had appointments in public health programs. Finally, note the special facilities offered, because certain research collections or lab facilities may be important to you.

The information in the guide is not limited to anthropologists working in academic departments. Many government agencies and museums are also indexed in the guide. The listing of these professionals can be useful for networking. The guide provides addresses for the individuals listed, and you might write them asking about their research or seeking their professional advice. Perhaps you are interested in learning about career opportunities in the National Park Service, for example. The guide lists about a hundred anthropologists who work for the service and could serve as contacts; many of them have only B.A.s. Most professionals are flattered to receive such inquiries and will be glad to give you information and advice—especially if you can be specific about your plans and what you need to know.

Specialty Guides

Anthropological associations specializing in a subfield of anthropology, such as archaeology, or a topic or region, such as ceramics or the former Yugoslavia, also publish guides to programs emphasizing those specialties. Many of these

---

What to Look for in a Graduate Program

_____ Good proportion of degrees awarded to grad students enrolled, indicating a low dropout rate

_____ Special program emphases such as museology, cultural resource management, forensics, or Asian studies

_____ Opportunities for field experience through professors' research grants or field schools

_____ Opportunities for income and tuition waivers through teaching and research assistantships

_____ Large number of predoctoral graduate students on their own grants

_____ Success in employment of its recent degree recipients

_____ Satisfaction of its current graduate students or recent degree recipients

_____ Quality of and access to the labs and research collections on campus and in nearby institutions

_____ Cost of living in the area and availability of off-campus jobs

_____ More than one full-time faculty member specializing in your interests

_____ No disabling schisms among faculty

---

guides are easily accessible on the Web. NAPA's applied anthropology guide to graduate programs, for example, is *www.anthap.oakland.edu/gradprog. htm*. Historical archaeologists should consult the Society for Historical Archeology's Web site, *www.sha.org/sha_col1.htm.* Other publications are mentioned in Chapter 8.

Graduate and Professional School Fairs

The four colleges in my region cohost an annual fair to which these colleges invite representatives of various graduate and professional training programs, such as international affairs, library science, and dentistry. Your career services office would know of such a fair in your region. These fairs provide excellent ways to browse over a wide variety of possibilities quickly, ask questions, and pick up literature or applications.

Campus Visits

Once you've got a few graduate programs picked out, there is no substitute for visiting their facilities and talking face-to-face with professors, financial aid officers, potential employers, and students. When you were high school juniors, many of you visited undergraduate institutions with your parents. Graduate school deserves at least as much care in selection as that.

WINNING ACCEPTANCE

What do you have to do to get accepted into the graduate program of your choice? What is the role of scores on the Graduate Record Exam (GRE), professors' recommendations, interviews, personal essays, your college grade-point average (GPA), and honors or accomplishments?

You need to find the answers to these questions for the specific institution you wish to attend. Variation is so great that there is no point in generalizing about the relative weight of these things. Some schools won't look at you unless you are an "A" student or exceed a specific GRE-score cutoff. Others are willing to give more weight to a good recommendation from a professor they know or some interesting project you've already done, like travel in Kenya or work in a drug rehabilitation center.

At the risk of sounding platitudinous, I make the following recommendations.

1. Earn good grades. Good grades in high school are the best predictor of success in college; the same holds true for college grades and graduate school.

2. Prepare for the GREs: there are workbooks that show you how the test is structured, complete with practice questions.

3. Participate in interesting extracurricular activities that develop skills.

4. Arrange for a personal interview at the graduate school, and prepare for it (see the box titled "What to Look for in a Graduate Program").

5. Write numerous drafts of your personal essay (e.g., "Describe your goals for graduate school, life, the universe, and why you think we should let a punk like you come here") so that you really say something true and interesting.

6. Ask a few people to critique that essay for you. A good guide to the essay can be found on Renssaeler Polytechnic Institute's Web page: *www.rpi. edu/web/writingcenter/gradapp.html.*

7. Select professors for recommendations carefully.

As for those recommendations, writing effective letters is a skill, and only some professors have it. Select a couple of good ones, and coach them on what to say. That is, remind them of the specific things you have done, with them or with other professors, that make you look like a good risk for graduate school.

In your own essay and in your professors' letters, what can you do or say to prove to anyone that you are mature, self-directed, moral, cooperative, hard-working, persistent, bright, creative, literate, et cetera? (*Aren't* you?)

PAYING FOR IT

It is true that if you are good enough for graduate school and someone there likes you, you should be able to get funding for tuition, books, and research—at least. Often a sum for living expenses is included, too. But frequently you must first prove that you're good enough and you must develop rapport with a professor. Anthropology departments, for example, have only a few dollars to attract the most promising new graduate students. They expect most of the other new students to get by in other ways at first. The departments tend to put most of their money into holding onto the second- and third-year students whom they like by offering them jobs assisting in research or teaching.

This is not to say that you cannot find ways to fund your first year or two. Holding a job while you go to graduate school is common. For example, my student Joe, heading off to graduate school in anthropology a couple of years ago, didn't get a scholarship at first, but the university helped him to find a job as a tutor and academic advisor for undergraduates. A few years earlier, Maryann paid most of her first-year bills in library science graduate school by serving as a dorm director.

Recent Ph.D.s report that about 50 percent of their graduate education was paid for by fellowships and assistantships. Another 25 percent was paid for by grants from federal agencies like the National Science Foundation. The other 25 percent was from the student's own pocket, usually through a job, sometimes on campus (Evans 1997: 17–18).

You may be eligible for support through a scholarship fund that you and the grad school of your choice are not even aware of yet. There are, for example, scholarships set up for all *kinds* of people. Being the grandchild of a red-haired Spanish Civil War veteran might actually be worth cash to you!

Government-subsidized loans are worth considering, too. Instead of taking a low-paying job that competes with your schoolwork and may slow down your completion of the degree, taking out a loan allows you to enroll full-time and defer interest until you finish the degree. Download the "Student Guide to Financial Aid" from the U.S. Department of Education Web page (*www.ed.gov/prog_info/SFA/StudentGuide/1998-9/index.html*).

Books on financial aid for education are numerous. Ask your librarian. When I did, I was given a list that included *Peterson's Grants for Graduate Students and Postdoctoral Study* (1995), *Graduate School Funding Handbook* (Vahle-Hamel, Morris-Heiberger, and Miller-Vick 1995), and Laurie Blum's *Free Money for Graduate School* (2000). Some of the career guidance Web sites mentioned in this book also have information about funding your graduate education.

STRATEGIES FOR SUCCESS IN GRADUATE SCHOOL

Recent recipients of Ph.D. degrees are surveyed every two years by the American Anthropological Association. Some of the more provocative questions asked are "Would you do it again?" and "Do you have any advice for the new graduate student?" Like undergraduate anthropology majors, most new Ph.D.s (85 percent) look back on choosing to go to graduate school at their particular institution as the right move (Givens, Evans, and Jablonski 1997: 17–18). Of course, only the successful degree recipients are surveyed. A number of their classmates have dropped out. Why? We don't have data on them. Some of the reasons I am aware of are family needs, poor health, poor relations with faculty supervisors, or landing a good job before finishing the degree.

Even more impressive than the fact that the successful have few regrets is this: even they are upset with their graduate schools for the poor or insufficient advice and help they received in developing their career path. They have some heartfelt advice for those who follow in their footsteps:

- Get an interdisciplinary education, combining anthropology with some other field. I have met such graduates with training in fields as varied as counseling, video communications, geographical information systems, and park management.

- Prepare for both academic and nonacademic careers. Archaeologists in government or the private sector, for example, are critical of their graduate training for failing to prepare them for handling the many legal, governmental, and public aspects of archaeology (Zeder 1997). Often one's graduate school professors don't know much about this either, but experience in internships will fill that gap.

- Develop your own network with other students and professors world-wide. According to the surveys, one's thesis supervisor may be a poor career mentor, but the network can take his or her place.

Professional anthropological associations have been offering more career guidance and internship opportunities to graduate students in recent years.

Applying for and Getting Admitted to Graduate School: Use Your Anthropology!

Selecting and gaining admission to the graduate school of your choice will be greatly aided if you just spend a little time using the skills you've acquired as an anthropology major.

Do Research   Accumulate data on colleges and universities offering programs in the fields that you prefer. Narrow the choice to about five. Write or call their admissions offices and *find out a person's name there*. Think about all of your contacts with this person as a series of open-ended interviews that you are conducting to obtain the necessary data on which to base conclusions. As with informants in any survey, the more you contact them, the greater help they will render you. Ask to be sent everything required to apply for the program, ask about an on-campus visit and interviews, and ask for the names and phone numbers of some recent alumni from the program you are interested in. (This may take a little while to arrange, but it is very worthwhile.)

Tune up Your Listening Skills   Always call from a comfortable, quiet spot, and have available paper and pencil to jot notes. If the program encourages or requires visits to the campus, find out whether it offers overnight lodging or aid for travel expenses. Do not be afraid to let them know that you are applying to other schools as well. While at the school, visit several different classes, especially if they are being taught by the professor you want to study with.

Use Personal Connections   If there are alumni from your preferred schools who are teaching at the college you now attend, even if they are not in the same department, get to know them to learn about the school and the community. Use the faculty in your own department also. Through electronic mail, you can correspond with a faculty member at your chosen program about his or her latest book, article, or project. Get a professor on your side.

The mentoring program directed by NAPA is an example (*www.anthap. oakland.edu*). The environmental internship sponsored by the SfAA and EPA has also been doing good work (*www.sfaa.net/eap/abouteap.html*). Up-to-date information on these organizations flows through their newsletters and e-mail discussion lists.

To test the ideas in this chapter, try Exercise 2, "Literature Survey"; Exercise 4, "Demography"; Exercise 7, "Life History"; and Exercise 8, "Internetworking."

CHAPTER 7

What Careers Do People with Anthropology B.A.s Pursue?

Some well-known and successful people have majored in anthropology. Novelists Kurt Vonnegut and Ursula Le Guin and cartoonist Gary Larsen (of the *Australopithecus* jokes) are examples (Neely 1998: 157). Ohio congressman Rob Portman, Barnes and Noble's founder Steve Riggio, and Motorola corporate lawyer Robert Faulkner are three more notables with a B.A. in anthropology.

If you accept the premise that what anthropology alumni are doing, you could do, then I have good news for you. Anthropology departments have conducted surveys of their alumni that consistently show that the work alumni are doing is highly varied, usually satisfying, and conducted with an anthropological sensibility. In this chapter I'll report on three such alumni surveys. Then we'll look at short biographies of some anthropology B.A. holders whose careers are instructive. Finally, I'll explain in very impressive language why neither you nor I can predict what path *you* will follow, but I will show you the map of some paths you might take.

THE NORTHEASTERN U.S. SURVEY, 1986

In a survey of anthropology alumni from colleges in the northeastern United States, my students Aimee Kratts and Clarissa Hunter sorted the 616 respondents' occupations into seventeen categories, as shown in Table 7.1.

Kratts and Hunter found that 62 percent of the alumni worked in the profit sector, 9 percent in the nonprofit sector, and 6 percent in government. The remaining 16 percent were currently students in graduate or professional school.

When asked to respond to the statement "My anthropological education helps me in my current work," 71 percent of the northeastern alumni replied

TABLE 7.1   Types of Occupations Held by Northeastern Anthropology Alumni

Management	19%	(Self-applied labels of manager, administrator, consultant,or director)
Student	16%	
Teacher or professor	10%	
Medicine	6%	(Doctor, nurse)
Communications, media	5%	(Editor, writer, reporter, television producer, cartoonist, model)
Business	5%	(Accountant, sales or marketing agent, insurance salesperson, stockbroker)
Other professionals	5%	(Public relations officer, librarian, landscape designer, architect, urban planner, geologist, clergy, transportation planner)
Law	4%	
Self-employed	4%	(Small-business owner, contractor)
Clerical	3%	
Research	3%	(All types)
Government agency	3%	
Computers, technology	2%	
Archaeology	2%	
Social work	2%	
Museums	1%	
Trades	1%	

Source: Kratts and Hunter 1986.

that they agreed or strongly agreed. Only 15 percent disagreed or strongly disagreed. A therapist commented,

> [In psychotherapy] understanding symbolic systems' effect on group consciousness and the effects of sociocultural values and norms on the individual is extremely valuable. Cultural determinants of body movement and expression are also fascinating to me.

A small-business owner found her work tapped her interest and skills in archaeology:

> I greatly enjoy my work operating an antique shop. All aspects of the business are satisfying: attending antique shows, unearthing an early

item, researching its age and provenance, restoring or repairing it, and educating a potential customer about it, as well as offering an appraisal service.

For those who go to graduate school in another field, the anthropology major is still often useful. A recent law school graduate who had studied physical anthropology and forensics with us sent an unsolicited e-mail testimonial recently to report:

> An anthropology degree was a very helpful prelude to law school. In anthropology, as in law, you must support your theory through logical arguments based on the available facts. This method of reasoning is the cornerstone of legal analysis. And I found that my [anthropology major] had prepared me well for the rigors of law school.

Most (81 percent) of the alumni surveyed claimed they were satisfied and challenged by their current work, and 74 percent felt their decision to major in anthropology was a good one. Men were slightly more satisfied with their current work and found their major slightly more applicable, which suggests that even in the last fifteen years women in the working world have not quite achieved parity.

A teacher of students with physical and mental handicaps commented that anthropology helps her to understand people so that she can do her job more effectively: "One learns that no matter how bizarre a behavior or culture may be, it's still *people* who are doing it; people exhibit behaviors, but they are not the behaviors themselves."

Some alumni waxed enthusiastic about anthropology as the foundation for a liberal arts education. A banker urged anthropology majors to be confident and ambitious:

> Go for it. No one in business will ever hold a liberal arts education against you. One can always make up trade courses in business subjects. Improving one's mind can only be done by exploring liberal arts subjects with an intellectual (serious) intent. In the long run, this will mark you as superior to a crowd of business students who never studied anything else.

Is he correct? Obviously *he's* more likely to hire a liberal arts student than other applicants. And he is not unique.

Some alumni felt anthropology's breadth makes it more adaptable than other fields. Wrote a child-support enforcement officer,

Anthropology advocates that the practitioner be well informed and capable in many social sciences as well as in anthropology and, in most cases, in a goodly number of the "hard" sciences. With this renaissance man/woman requirement, more competencies and capabilities are exhibited by the anthropologist than other social scientists.

A social services manager agreed that anthropology gives him the holistic perspective to understand the world better and to do his job more effectively.

I work as a management analyst in a county social services agency. Although it is difficult to get an anthropology *degree* recognized as relevant, the anthropological approach is, I feel, one of the best for this sort of job. I'm always . . . translating, from computer programmers to social workers, from line and staff to administration, from counseling services to community forums. . . . I do human resource planning and projection, program evaluations, office space design with architects (again, *translating* social work needs into office layout), and I develop management tools for social work and welfare managers. I am the only person doing this work in a department of two hundred.

The manager is convinced his breadth and special perspective are respected. He continued,

The reward comes from the deep appreciation that staff and administrators have for the approach that I take. They prefer an anthropologist to an MBA, MPA [Master of Public Administration], or a narrowly educated evaluation specialist, which are the typical fields that qualify applicants for this job.

What these remarks by alumni suggest to me is that these people majored in anthropology because its fundamental concepts and methods for understanding human behavior matched their deeply ingrained personal predispositions. After college, they found satisfying employment in positions where those same predispositions—now more developed through the major—were welcome and useful.

That conclusion supports a *self-discovery theory of college;* that is, college is not a place where you learn what you need to know to get a job, but rather a place where you discover what tasks you're good at and the tasks you enjoy, and then expand your ability to do those tasks for a living.

THE NORTH CAROLINA SURVEY, 1988

A survey similar to the northeastern one but conducted a few years later with 126 anthropology alumni only a few years out of six colleges and universities in North Carolina found the same moderately high level of satisfaction with current occupations and the same moderate level of applicability of the anthropology training (Tefft, Harris, and Godwin 1988).

A quarter of the North Carolina alumni had found positions in business, 18 percent in teaching, and the others were in many government, medical, and service fields. Almost half went to graduate school immediately, but only 31 percent of those continued in anthropology. Although the respondents had been out of college five years or less, almost half reported changing jobs two or three times since graduating. (This mobility, which is also very common in the northeastern alumni data, confirms what I have read: liberal arts majors hunt around for a few years, finding out what options exist and homing in on work that matches their interests and skills—in other words, learning *after* receiving their diplomas what this workbook helps you learn *before* you graduate.)

About half of the North Carolina alumni believed that their current position did not use their anthropological training, but on the other hand, their major didn't hurt them in getting that position. They did report that their more general liberal arts skills were useful: leadership, critical thinking, problem solving, working without close supervision, decision making, report writing, and creativity. If they could repeat their college career, most North Carolina alumni, like their northeastern peers, would be an anthropology major again, but they would also take some courses that were more directly geared to their current work in business, management, science, and so on. Alumni also recommended internships and other practical experience while still in college.

THE PLATTSBURGH SURVEY, 1993

As part of its department review, SUNY Plattsburgh's anthropology program investigated where its recent graduates were working. In his final report, the chair, James Armstrong, found that besides those who had entered good graduate programs in anthropology and other fields, many B.A. holders had entered into social-change or social-service positions:

> Two of our students are in the Peace Corps, four are working as professional archaeologists, one is an educator with AIDS Council of Northern New York, two are alcoholism counselors, two are working as case workers in homeless shelters, two are working in community residences, one is the deputy director of an agency that serves developmentally disabled individuals, one is the social science research coordinator for Earth Watch, and one is an administrative assistant with Teachers for Social Responsibility.

PROFILES OF FIVE PEOPLE WITH B.A.S IN ANTHROPOLOGY

Let's zoom in from the statistical overview to some short biographies of individual anthropology majors. These five people were selected because I have taught them or met them and I consider their career paths and current work interesting. I doubt they are especially representative of all anthropology majors, given that they were all good students and each completed graduate training eventually, though few in anthropology. As you read these profiles, see if you notice any patterns.

Energy

Tom's undergraduate research project at the University of California, Santa Cruz, in the mid-1980s involved action anthropology with an organic farming community that was rapidly becoming an industry. Tom helped to develop the California Organic Foods Act of 1990 and marketing institutions, such as a weekly price report, that have since helped the industry to thrive.

When Tom finished his coursework in 1986, he was sure he didn't want to teach. So he put off graduation to pursue a decidedly less cerebral career: electrical contracting. After working as an electrician for seven years, he finished his B.A. thesis and returned to school to earn a certificate in energy management and design at Sonoma State University. With his specialized training he ratcheted up his contracting work to consulting work with a focus on energy conservation in buildings. In six years he rose to senior consultant/analyst in a statistics and engineering research firm. Realizing where the action was, he found time for a second certificate, in market research methods, and then a third, in marketing planning. Then in 1998 he joined two coworkers, both software-savvy energy engineers, to form GeoPraxis, Inc. (*www.geopraxis.com*). GeoPraxis's primary mission is "to transform how people manage and conceptualize their use of resources, particularly energy. We are a growing, profitable business with an explicit culture change agenda."

Clearly, anthropology is still front and center in Tom's work. He describes himself in professional publications as an applied anthropologist who draws on his formal training in research methods to improve resource sustainability in agricultural production and energy consumption. He designs and evaluates marketing programs intended to accelerate the adoption of more resource-efficient technologies and behaviors. His résumé emphasizes that this unique approach to qualitative research in the energy services industry relies on "expertise in the techniques of ethnographic interviewing and participant observation." He also uses a variety of survey instruments and conducts focus groups, both in person and on-line.

I heard Tom present a paper on his consultancy with a recent GeoPraxis client. An electric utility, Jamaica Public Service, acquired Inter-American Development Bank funds to invite him to survey energy use on that Caribbean island and to recommend conservation measures. Working closely with a local contractor, he interviewed end users, observed their activities, talked shop with local engineers, and conducted a formal survey. Gathering this market information is where his anthropology came to the fore, Tom reports. He learned, for example, that many of the island's imported air conditioners and refrigerators are incompatible with the local electrical system, and many are highly inefficient. He also found that demand for residential electrical appliances is rising rapidly, far ahead of utility projections. He recommended continued support of new appliance labeling standards and training of installation contractors.

Tom's recent clients include corporations, public utilities, and government agencies in California, Texas, Arizona, Indiana, Massachusetts, and elsewhere. New GeoPraxis projects include Web sites to help homeowners choose efficient new appliances and software that allows architects to predict energy performance of a new building while it is still in the computer design phase. He has relied on his talents in software, electrical systems, and marketing to serve an applied anthropological goal.

Waste

Glenn began college with an interest in classical archaeology, but contract work in CRM and fieldwork with me in pollution disaster impacts nudged him toward environmental issues. He gained useful experience as a teaching assistant in a summer environmental studies workshop. He also founded and edited the anthropology club newsletter, "The Excavator."

Glenn's interest in the environment and social change led him to Goddard College for an M.A. in social ecology, a field oriented to identifying the cultural practices, beliefs, and social structures that shape our environmental relations. Two years later, degree in hand, Glenn moved to Philadelphia, where he felt prospects might be good because he had made a number of contacts while conducting research on social change movements there as part of his master's work at Goddard. Using his ethnographic skills of research and interviewing, he sniffed out grassroots organizations dedicated to environmental justice. Soon he found one eager to employ solar and energy-efficiency technology to address the needs of low-income communities. Working with the group, he found his niche as a creator and organizer of nonprofit organizations.

After four years, Glenn returned to Vermont to help establish the Institute for Social Ecology as an independent educational organization. In short order he became involved in statewide efforts to improve the management and organizational capacity of nonprofit organizations working in the state. In this effort he was recruited to professionalize a statewide coalition working on recycling and solid waste reduction efforts. As executive director of the Association of Vermont Recylers, he shepherded boards of directors, hob-nobbed with trash collectors, wrote grants and newsletters, lobbied, and led meetings. His adaptability as an ethnographer was essential: "You learn on the job. Organizations have a culture that you can figure out, map, and shape. As a member of governing boards, as a director of organizations, and as a consultant, I did constant fieldwork."

In the late 1980s, Glenn shifted from working on ordinary solid waste to specializing in medical waste. He met Hollie, a nurse who was questioning the culture of her hospital organization. While providing excellent health care, the hospital generated large volumes of waste, some of it hazardous, which became a community health problem. Together, Glenn and Hollie formed a consulting firm, CGH Environmental Strategies, Inc., in Burlington, Vermont. "Again I had to do lots of research. I was able to learn the technical side of types of waste and their proper management, but it was much more difficult to learn the culture of how a hospital actually works. For that I married my chief informant, who had twenty years of experience as a member of the inner 'tribe.'"

At first, Glenn and Hollie started slowly, holding onto their day jobs. Over time, their consulting firm found clients all over the United States willing to pay for consultations and workshops. Lately they have expanded into the U.S. Virgin Islands, Central America, the Philippines, Thailand, and India.

"Going into the work with an open mind and a willingness to listen and observe set us apart from other consultants, aid agencies, and salesmen." Glenn found his anthropological training valuable, helping him to analyze organizations, conduct participant observation, write well, and hold his judg-ments in check.

Along the way, Glenn has made time to complete a Ph.D. in anthropol-ogy at the Union Institute in Cincinnati, Ohio. He urges students interested in following in his footsteps to

find a nonprofit management course. Many new graduates will work at least part of their career in a nonprofit agency. Organizations are cul-tural constructs. Understanding more about how such groups work will assist you in deciding how to use your skills better in that organization and how to explain the relevance of your skills. It takes away the need to defend anthropology to your clients or future employer.

Historic Preservation

Heather knew before she received her B.A. in anthropology that she wanted to work in museums and historical archaeology. She sought every opportunity to gain experience in college and during the summer. She volunteered at a museum near her home and at the anthropology museum on our campus. She won a summer fellowship to a museum of early American history in Massachusetts and also served as an intern analyzing the old silver collections at our county historical association. When she graduated in 1995, she enrolled in the University of Delaware's M.A. program in American history with a certificate in museum studies. The faculty knew her because she had attended the university for a semester through the National Student Exchange Program. In graduate school, too, she found practical experience as an intern in publications, teaching, conserving early manuscripts, and constructing exhibits, both on campus and in the region's museums and historic sites.

Two years later, as a new M.A., Heather found through her professors a curatorial internship at a historic park in Philadelphia.

> The interview [for the internship] showed me two things. First is the importance of networking. The curator at this museum had worked with the professor who directed my internship last summer, *and* the previous intern was a classmate of mine in a summer museum fellowship. Second, I learned that during an interview you are also interviewing the interviewer to decide whether you're a good match and want to work for them.

As assistant curator she conducted research on the city's immigrant history and also provided documentary background for an archaeology dig. When funding for the internship evaporated after a year, she learned through her local professional grapevine that the Preservation Alliance for Greater Philadelphia was about to receive a large grant to provide technical assistance and funding for the three hundred historic structures and sites in the area. Heather had planned to be a museum curator, but she thought grantsmanship would be a useful skill, so she applied for a staff position. She became project assistant for a two-person staff of the Heritage Investment Program, an initiative of the Pew Charitable Trusts. Her office coordinates workshops, offers site visits and assessments, and serves as a clearinghouse of information for historic sites that are open to the public.

In her current position Heather edits the program's newsletter, reviews grants and helps societies to write them ("I've acquired skills in reading budgets and balance sheets"), and maintains the membership database. She is helping organize a national conference in 2001. Recently she was the project coordinator of a copublished guide that lists historic sites and cultural institutions available to lease for special events. She has been able to "draw upon many skills I gained while an anthropology major, including interviewing techniques, research, and publication editing." She enjoys the publicizing, coordinating, organizing workshops, and solving problems so much now that she's altered her career goals to include administration of historic sites. Her advice to current anthropology majors: "Read and live by [this book]. It was very helpful in my interview preparation. They *will* ask the question of how your degree in anthropology will benefit your work as an employee. My current boss asked me that in my interview!"

Health

Rachna completed college in 1995 with a B.A. in cultural anthropology, a strong science background, and an abiding interest in shaping health policy. She was an honors student but found time to gain valuable experience as an intern conducting a survey for the community services agency in town. She also volunteered at a hospital and at a teen pregnancy counseling center, presented a paper at a regional anthropology meeting, and served as an officer in several organizations.

When her parents moved to Pittsburgh that summer, Rachna followed. "I knew that the job market in Pittsburgh was fairly good, so I didn't settle for any job; I wanted one I'd enjoy and gain valuable experience from." She applied to the natural history division of Carnegie Museums. There she was cautioned that positions were highly competitive, but she was persistent, making follow-up calls to the key people. A few weeks later, she was hired by the planning and development department of the museum. Her tasks involved fund-raising, organizing premieres of new exhibits, and recruiting museum guides and volunteers.

While at the museum, Rachna investigated graduate schools in medical anthropology and health care public policy. "I learned from people at the museum that Carnegie Mellon University (CMU) had a great health care policy and management program at its Heinz School." She was accepted by CMU in January 1996 and began classes part-time while continuing full-time at the museum. Then, realizing she needed to concentrate on her studies, she switched to full-time student status and part-time at the museum for another year. Then she resigned from her job and attended school full-time for a year, receiving her M.S. degree in 1998.

During that year Rachna again launched a search—this time for employment. "Our grad school had an excellent career center and good counselors." Her applications for jobs in several federal agencies, think tanks, and private health care consulting firms yielded three job offers. She chose the General Accounting Office (GAO), a legislative bipartisan agency that acts as the watchdog of federal programs. "I picked GAO because it was addressing both public policy and health care policy work." She became a health care auditor in the Health, Education, and Human Services Division in downtown Washington, D.C.

> I was responsible for conducting research and writing reports and preparing testimony for congressional staff. I realized that . . . research, public speaking, conducting interviews, designing surveys—all these skills that I had learned as an anthropology major were finally paying off.

Eighteen months later, Rachna took another leap. "I was ready to face greater challenges." She learned about private consulting from some of her work friends. Her applications to all the leading health care consulting firms in the Washington, D.C., region resulted within a month in an offer from one of the biggest. In her present position, "we are currently reviewing the financial cost reports for Medicare patients for the federal Health Care Financing Administration, which formulates policy for Medicare. I travel frequently. My first project is for three weeks in Louisville, Kentucky. Then I'm off to New York City."

Aliens, Far and Near

Richard began college in 1989 as an art major at the University of Florida but found the field too culturally narrow. He discovered anthropology by taking a class and initially directed his energies to cave art and archaeology. By the time he completed his M.A. in cultural anthropology in 1996, his interests had shifted to displaced populations and culture loss or change. Through his professors Richard located an internship with the International Rescue Committee, in Altanta, Georgia. The six-month internship evolved into a two-year position. "I was program coordinator, grant writer, case worker, and computer guy." He interviewed refugees about how households operated in their home country and in the United States to develop a cultural-orientation program for new arrivals. He worked long hours and, as a case worker, was intimately

Trickster character Bea, her friends, and her archenemy, the creations of Richard Interlandi, M.A., anthropology. © 2000 Richard D. Interlandi.

involved in many families' lives. "And people count on you. It can be hard, but also uplifting. You meet people who have gone through events you can barely imagine yet retain this positive attitude." After two years he returned to his fiancée in Florida and started up a Web consulting firm with some friends. His anthropological interests have shaped his current work. "I get design ideas from all kinds of art." His experience in writing has been valuable, and some of his marketing ideas derive from theoretical anthropology. He continues to volunteer time to nonprofit organizations. Richard still wants to earn a Ph.D. in anthropology, but he is currently being well paid to do interesting computer work, so the plan is on hold.

Upon returning to Florida, Richard revived his drawing skills and mixed them with anthropology, creating a delightful comic strip on the Web called smallgreY (*www.smallgrey.com*) about a set of characters on Mars. The characters' remarks and adventures mirror our culture's foibles. The art is pure Richard, but the wit is informed by anthropology and by his Atlanta experience with people who were coping with an alien culture. He is also finishing a comic book about a trickster character, drawing on cross-cultural studies of this troublemaking yet sympathetic figure.

The comic book is about a hero of sorts, Bea (half bee, half human-like), who lives in a garden. She protects the garden's good-natured inhabitants with a combination of wisdom, trickery, and magical powers. The first book is about a mutant pea/scarecrow who desires to claim the garden as his own peadom.

These freelance projects will, he hopes, finance the future doctoral degree.

Patterns

Commonalities in these five profiles may serve as advice to the reader. Most of my informants acquired valuable extracurricular experience in college. Internships were helpful. The importance of networks is clear. Informants have combined long-standing talents—artistic, organizational, or computational, for example—with skills picked up in formal education, including but not limited to their anthropology major. There is more than one path to acquiring degrees. Some informants went straight through school, as Heather did, whereas others picked up their credentials along the way, as Tom and Glenn did. Some have a boss and a salary, as Rachna does, and others are their own bosses, as Richard is. Finally, keep in mind that these are snapshots in the year 2000; by 2010, no doubt, these dynamic people may be doing something quite different, and although we can't predict what it will be, in retrospect it will undoubtedly make sense.

YOUR CAREER AND CHAOS THEORY

Sven Newman's *So, What* Are *You Doing After College?* (1995) is an inspiring and entertaining collection of essays by liberal arts graduates in many fields today. What is striking is the zigzagging and usually surprising paths these young men and women took to arrive at their current work. We see that zigzag in some of the profiles above.

Modern chaos theory describes such a career path quite well. In chaos theory, we begin with a simple-looking equation and a starting value and then feed the result of the equation back into it as the next starting point. Soon the results become technically unpredictable from the starting value. Similarly, we can define your starting conditions (your B.A. and college career) and we can write the equation that describes the process (networking, plus study, multiplied by experience, etc.), but when you feed the results of one career step back into the equation for the next step, and repeat that a few times, soon you are in a place that is truly unpredictable. *Seven Life Lessons of Chaos,* by John Briggs and F. David Peat (1999), is an entertaining extension of this idea into the self-help literature.

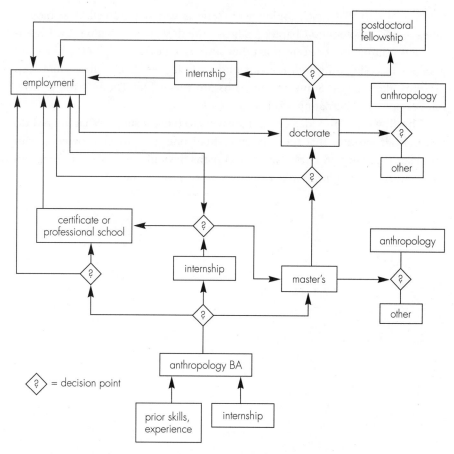

FIGURE 7.1   How Anthropologists Get to That First Good Job

Your career from this point forward may be chaotic—that is, unpredictable—but that doesn't mean that your prospects aren't bright. The statistics that create a collective picture of where job seekers end up are clear enough. The U.S. Department of Education reported a study revealing that two years after graduating, 66 percent of 1993 college graduates were working full-time. Many of the others were in graduate school. Of those employed, 75 percent were in fields related to their major field of study, and 75 percent viewed their current position as having career potential (American Federation of Teachers 1997).

A FLOWCHART

A chaotic or unpredictable process doesn't mean that it's out of your control. There is a pattern to the choices that people with B.A.s in anthropology have made to get to that first position with serious career potential. The biographies in this chapter and Chapter 3 suggest the flowchart in Figure 7.1. Undergraduates start at the bottom (don't they always?), developing their talents and interests in college through courses and experiences. Each subsequent step presents alternatives. Some of the paths are reversible. There is the option, for example, of alternating work with study.

This flowchart provides general answers to the question "What might I do next?" It also shows that there is more than one path to employment with promise. There are probably two dozen paths through these steps to employment, and I've known people who have trod most of them.

CHAPTER 8

How Do I Begin a Job-Hunting Campaign?

Hunting for a job resembles gaining entrée into the field site to begin ethnography. That is, you have to decide where to go, who can help you get there, and how to present yourself when you arrive. The task of finding out what kind of work you want to do, where, and with whom, is a course of study in itself. Why wait until you graduate to begin that study? The second- or third-year student can research the options, and the fourth-year student can take several steps toward finding that first employer.

The career services office at your school is a valuable resource. Students think of that office as a place to sign up for on-campus interviews or to scan index cards of available jobs that have been posted on a bulletin board. How depressing! But if your career center is like mine, it offers a whole range of services, including counseling in matching yourself to a career, maintaining a library of career literature and workbooks, offering workshops on how to get hired and how to compose résumés and letters, and arranging internships. The center usually also offers guidance in interviewing, dossier building, and shadowing (see Exercise 3, "Participant Observation"). Such services would cost hundreds of dollars if you engaged them on the open market.

Your full use of career services gives you a competitive edge. At my college, a survey of alumni showed that 91 percent who used the full services of the career center were employed or in graduate school, compared to 70 percent who used no services or just a few walk-in ones (*SUNY Career Services Annual Report 1989–90*).

Besides working with career counselors, I recommend undertaking two interrelated job-hunting activities: becoming informed and building a network.

BECOMING INFORMED

This shouldn't be the only book you work with in preparing your career search. The university library and career services office have a collection of manuals. I have browsed the shelves in the big chain bookstores and found other good books alongside less useful works with titles like *Killer Cover Letters* and *Hot Jobs in Tulip Speculation*. I recommend two books that offer sound advice based on the authors' long experience and that reinforce my main points. *What Color Is Your Parachute? 2000,* by Richard Nelson Bolles (1999), has good exercises on self-assessment and expertly punctures a number of cultural myths about the career search process. Howard Figler's *The Complete Job-Search Handbook* (1999) is very positive about the value of a liberal education. Figler shows you how to rephrase your accomplishments, both to yourself and to potential employers, which is the process of "transcultural self-presentation" I have described in this book. He has recently been invited to give workshops at anthropology conferences.

Learn how to read job announcements and begin to research the market early in your degree program. As I'll explain in the next chapter, sending résumés in response to published ads isn't the best way to find a job. But studying job announcements will reveal what skills and experience are widely sought. Take the last two years of your college career to acquire those skills. Perform Exercise 14, "Interpreting the Text," to gain some market intelligence.

Next, put yourself in the information flow, which entails joining, subscribing, and attending. There are two streams in this flow: one deriving from anthropology and the other deriving from the field you are interested in, such as education, medicine, social services, resource preservation, museums, and so on. I'll mention some joining, subscribing, and attending you should attempt in the anthropology stream. Your professors can suggest similar efforts in the field-specific stream.

Join

In 2000, a basic student membership in the AAA is $60, membership in the Association of Physical Anthropology is $55, and membership in the Society of American Archaeology is $55. Membership in AAA, for example, entitles you to join one of AAA's sections, such as the National Association of Practicing Anthropologists (NAPA) or the National Association of Student Anthropologists (NASA). Other sections may be joined for a small fee. In addition, join a regional association, like the Northeastern Anthropological Association or the High Plains Anthropological Society. The regional organizations are inexpensive to join, usually independent and informal, welcome student participation, and have affordable annual meetings not too far from you.

Subscribe

The primary news organ for anthropology is *Anthropology News,* published monthly except during the summer (see Works Cited for details on this and all publications). There is a section on positions available, and there are frequent articles about the job market and related career help. Equally important are the reports from the many units of the American Anthropological Association: the Society for the Anthropology of Europe, the Culture and Agriculture unit, and the Society for Anthropology in Museums unit, to name a few. The reports contain names of practitioners, schools teaching the subject, places people are working, announcements of workshops to help professionals, and accounts of the adventures of practitioners at work. Archaeologists read the *SAA Newsletter,* containing the same sort of information, and biological anthropologists read the *Physical Anthropology News (PAN).* Applied anthropologists read the *SfAA Newsletter.* Subscriptions are included with membership; some newsletters can be ordered separately.

A useful little booklet for the M.A. and Ph.D. job hunter is *State Job Opportunities for Anthropologists* (Givens 1986). It explains how and where state job openings are defined, advertised, and won, with an attention to differences among states. Jobs that mesh well with anthropology are described. A simple listing of state jobs open to those with an M.A. in anthropology fills seven pages. Examples are urban planner, public information specialist, technical writer, placement counselor, criminologist, museum administrator, social worker, and safety engineer.

Also useful for those intending to apply their anthropology outside of academia is the Society for Applied Anthropology, whose quarterly publication, *Practicing Anthropology,* is packed with names of anthropologists doing interesting work, as well as the names of the organizations they are working in. For anthropology majors planning to teach in the public schools, I recommend the *Anthropology and Education Quarterly,* published by the Council on Anthropology and Education, and *AnthroNotes,* published by the Smithsonian Institution. Medical anthropologists, legal anthropologists, Africanists, and primatologists, among others, have their journals and newsletters. Your professor is probably regularly receiving others. Additional serial publications are mentioned in Chapter 4.

Besides printed news, there is the information superhighway, the Internet. "Anthro-L" is one of several discussion groups dedicated to discussion of everything about anthropology: upcoming conferences, theoretical arguments, positions available, giving and getting advice. Others are Humbio-L and Arch-L. Many of the discussants are graduate students, so it is an excellent forum for inquiring about graduate school: which school is good for

Iberian studies, or forensics? Tips on graduate school survival strategies? Financial assistance opportunities? Where are the contract archaeology jobs this year? Information is abundant, uncensored (and unverified!), and customized to you. A long list of anthropology discussion groups can be found at *http://home.worldnet.fr/~clist/Anthro/Texts/e-mail.html*.

In addition to discussion groups, most specialty fields within anthropology maintain Web sites that act as newsletters. Some are updated frequently enough to be a helpful news source for that field. In linguistics, for instance, two news and information sites are *www.emich.edu/~linguist* and *www.linguist.org*. Exercise 12, "Internetworking," samples some of the information on-line today.

Attend

Once you join an organization, such as the Southern Anthropological Society or the Committee of Anthropologists Concerned about AIDS, for example, you should go to their seasonal get-togethers, known in the jargon as meetings. The point is not to listen to academics read research papers (sometimes the *dullest* part of any meeting) but to meet the people doing the interesting work, catch the latest news, figure out what's in fashion now, and buy some of the best and most recent books at a discount. There usually is a panel or workshop on career development. Exercise 3, Part 1, "Participant Observation: Attending a Meeting," will give some structure to your first meetings.

BUILDING A NETWORK

Becoming informed is fairly passive, a matter of putting yourself in the way of the information stream. Building a network, however, is more active and, as we'll see in the next chapter, is one of the most important steps you can take to get a job. Besides tapping into information about the work world and job openings, building a network is the way to gain rapport with potential employers or with key informants who may know someone who is looking for someone just like you. Try Exercise 6, "Social-Network Analysis," to assess your connections.

Many of the activities I have advocated will help you build your network. Going to meetings, volunteering, and interning are all excellent ways to meet people. Also, correspondence and telephone conversations, office interviews, and Exercise 3, Part 2, "Participant Observation: Shadowing a Professional," are good ways to make helpful connections.

The National Student Exchange (NSE) is a good way to build a network. Many schools are members of NSE or similar consortia that permit students to study at a different institution or in a different part of the country for little or no extra cost over their home campus. Students may participate for a semester or a whole academic year.

Through a student exchange you may learn from and impress another group of professors, work in another college's museum or labs, meet graduate students (your home institution may not have them), and look into the graduate program at your host institution. In such cooperative programs, credit transfer is usually smooth. Plan ahead: your application must be approved by your campus coordinator by March of the school year before the one you intend to be away.

Each subfield of anthropology—linguistics, physical anthropology, cultural anthropology, and archaeology—has a slightly different network. For archaeologists, the State Historic Preservation Office (SHPO) is a potential network connection; the SHPO should be able to advise you about institutions and firms in your area that may be hiring for contract archaeology projects. Your state archaeologist, often associated with the state museum, can also supply you with the names of many private archaeological firms. The contact persons for the SHPO and state archaeologist are either familiar to your professors or can be located in state directories in your library.

If you are ready to begin the job search, then you will be well served by Exercise 3, Part 2, "Shadowing a Professional;" Exercise 5, "Transcultural Self-Presentation;" Exercise 6, "Social-Network Analysis;" Exercise 11, Part 2, "Working with Key Informants;" and Exercise 12, "Interview Yourself."

How Do I Get Hired?

THE RULES OF "THE HIRING GAME"

Getting hired is an excellent exercise in ethnographic research, because the process involves achieving entrée, seeking rapport, and bicultural fluency. You have to learn the implicit and unrecognized rules of a certain subculture (the employer's), which is different from your own (the colleges). The employer operates within a social structure that grows out of rules and values that you must quickly discover and key into. Much of what I report below comes from "Finding Your Employer and Getting Hired" (Career Planning Office, SUNY Potsdam, handout, n.d.).

From a cultural perspective, there is no uniform code of employer behavior, so an excessively formulaic approach to finding work—like mailing out two hundred résumés to the personnel offices of organizations you've never visited in person—is just flailing. Each organization has its own way, which is a mixture of habit, interpretations of federal guidelines, selective borrowing from each other's good ideas, and temporary fixes, so you have to figure out the way the one you want to work for does it.

Nevertheless, there are three generalizations worth making. First, for all but the biggest, most bureaucratized employers, it is fair to predict that the hiring process is an interruption in the work routine, just as attending to the anthropologist's needs can be a distraction in the informants' village. Therefore, the job seeker must demonstrate courteous persistence in courting the employer. Second, people prefer to hire someone they know, so if they've met you or you've swept floors for them as a volunteer, you have an advantage. And third, the employer wants commitment. Your college transcript and major, which seemed so important for the last four years, aren't enough. You must show evidence of commitment to the career as part of your self-interpretation. In anthropological terms, before they'll tell you important things, the natives want to know why you picked their village.

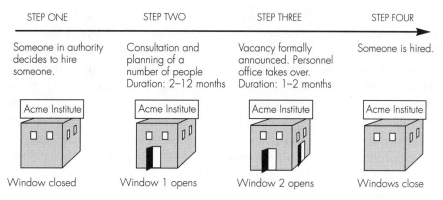

FIGURE 9.1   The Window Principle in Hiring

An etic analysis of the hiring process taught to me by *my* key informant (James Barrick, personal communication, October 12, 1993) reveals that many employers follow "the window principle." There are in fact two windows, or times of opportunity, in the hiring process. The process is illustrated in Figure 9.1. Being aware of this sociocultural pattern is to your advantage. Even though window 2 seems like the usual place for you to enter the process, it is only about two months long and *only about 20 percent of the jobs are filled then*. Of the jobs to be filled by college graduates, 80 percent are either filled or have a front-runner in window 1, before step 3 begins. To paraphrase my informant, "You don't have to be a math major to figure out which window to use."

It looks like the massive advance of the Internet isn't going to upset the window principle. In 1997, 20 percent of U.S. employers were recruiting by Internet, but only 1 percent of new hires were found that way (*Faculty Newsbytes,* October 1997). Even if the numbers have tripled by the time you read this, I expect that twenty-to-one ratio to remain constant.

Increase your chances of entering through window 1 by conducting Exercise 13, "Building Rapport with a Potential Employer."

HOW THE PROS FIND JOBS: NETWORKS AGAIN

Evidence that window 1 is the place to look for work comes from research conducted among professional anthropologists. In 1989 Charity Goodman and Liane Rosenblatt conducted a survey of the members of the Washington Area Practicing Anthropologists (WAPA) and reported their results in a paper titled "Applied Anthropologists and the Job Market: Strategies for Attaining Employment" (1991).

The members of WAPA have master's and doctor's degrees in anthropology and are working in the Washington, D.C., area. In 1967, 35 percent of WAPA members held nonacademic employment, but by 1987 the figure was 45 percent and rising. Almost all (95 percent) of the respondents to the survey were working in nonacademic settings. Because they worked in the Washington, D.C., area, it is not surprising that a little over 40 percent had positions in government, 20 percent in nonprofit foundations, and only 14 percent in for-profit companies. See the box titled "Job Titles of Anthropologists."

Notice that only four of the thirty-six titles listed in the box contain the words *anthropologist* or *archaeologist*. This is a reminder that, ethnosemantically speaking, the categories used by the tribe of practicing professionals are not the categories used by the professorial tribe.

Now we come to the main reason for reporting this piece of research: the most important strategy these professionals had for obtaining their position was *networking,* which means they entered at window 1, as described previously. For example, 41 percent said networking was paramount in winning their first job. Another 20 percent were even more creative than their networking colleagues: they entered at window 1 by creating their own job. In other words, they spoke with the key people and convinced them that there was a task that needed to be done and identified themselves as the ones to do it. Only 24 percent got their first jobs in window 2. They answered ads and sent in applications in the conventional manner. Almost the same strategies were used when respondents got their current work, which was the second or third position for some. Overall, 61 percent of the WAPA members responding to the survey identified networking as the most successful job-search strategy. This finding is no fluke. A survey of recent Ph.D.s reports that 44 percent found their job through networking (Givens, Evans, and Jablonski 1997: 318).

So, there is no reason to be cynical about the fact that "it's who you know." As an anthropologist you are well trained to get to know whom you need to know.

When asked to reflect on their job searches, most of the WAPA respondents concluded that self-definition is vital. As an anthropologist, they said, you have to work a little harder than some professionals do to define yourself as a professional with distinctive skills and to show anthropology's utility in the organization.

WAPA members' anthropological abilities were certainly used in their current work. The most commonly mentioned were quantitative methods, perception of the culture of the workplace, writing, interviewing, program-evaluation skills, and ethnographic and archaeological research.

Job Titles of Anthropologists

Respondents of WAPA Survey, 1989

Adjunct professor

Agriculture monitor and evaluator, international development branch

Anthropologist

Anthropologist and historic preservation planner

Archaeologist

Associate for research and management

Consultant

Criminal justice analyst and police specialist

Deputy commissioner for nutrition and health education

Director, Southeast Asian Resources project

Director of museum

Director of research

Editor

Environmental specialist

Freelance writer and teacher

Head, purchasing and technical support department

Management analyst

Marketing director

Midlevel government manager

Professional assistant

Program coordinator

Project manager

Project officer, natural resources management

Regional director, office of public housing

Research analyst

Research assistant professor

Research faculty member

Science and diplomacy fellow

Senior consultant in cultural resource management

Senior social scientist

Social anthropologist

Social science analyst

Socioeconomist

Special assistant to the deputy administrator for policy

Substance abuse counselor

Survey research supervisor

Source: Goodman and Rosenblatt 1991.

INTERPRETING A JOB ANNOUNCEMENT

Okay, class: another linguistics lesson. Yes, it will be on the test. Learning to parse the language in job announcements can reveal what the employer is really looking for. Knowing this, you can draft a more effective cover letter. If you're not entering the market yet, you'll discover what attributes you should acquire and display to become competitive.

Reading job ads can be a dismaying experience if you are unfamiliar with this context. It seems like the employer is asking for someone who can walk on water. It seems like you'll never get started because everyone wants three to five years' experience. But the employer isn't always prepared to pay the ideal candidate what he or she expects, or the ideal candidates simply aren't available at the moment. So there's *your* dossier, rising closer to the top of the pile.

Colleagues' stories, such as those in Chapters 3 and 7, as well as my own experience hiring academics, suggest two conclusions about job ads as "text."

- There are many clues in the telegraphically brief language of an announcement that reveal how the employer sees itself and what it wants to achieve through this hire. You need to do some close reading (and preferably some additional investigation), identify what is really needed and what are the culturally charged concepts, and then be sure to address them.
- The employer advertises in good faith, but who is actually hired usually does not match the ad language exactly. That is, successful applicants may not have all the qualifications advertised as "preferred" or "desirable," but may instead have other talents that the employer decides (or can be convinced) are equally valuable.

For example, when my department meets to define ideal candidates for a position, we usually agree on the "required" criteria we'll publish, such as the degree earned and the subfield specialty, without which a candidate will not make the first cut. We tend less often to agree on the "desirable" criteria, such as the amount of prior teaching experience and whether the candidate needs to teach a certain course. And then there are unpublished criteria that grow in importance once we have a short list, such as how well the candidate can motivate undergraduates or whether the candidate has some good ideas for funding the lab.

Many announcements will require or prefer three to five years of experience, which looks intimidating to holders of new degrees. If the language is "require," then probably the position demands more than a neophyte can offer. The position is likely a "replacement" job, because someone was doing the work but has left and the employer wants someone to come in and pick up right away. The employer is unable or unwilling to provide training to a beginner. Nevertheless, as you learn more about the position, you may have justification to negotiate. This is particularly true if the language is "prefer." Emphasize and illustrate your ability to learn quickly and with minimal supervision. Offer alternative experience. For example, between your two years of part-time volunteer work in a related activity at the university and your full-time internship one summer or semester, you may convince the employer that you've had sufficient preparation. Add to that experience a couple of your skills that they hadn't mentioned, which—you point out—will also be useful, such as youth counseling at summer camp, supervising a dig, or fluency in Spanish, and you may get around that experience barrier.

For practice in reading and replying to job postings, try Exercise 14, "Interpreting the Text." For further guidance in reading job postings, consult the manuals described in Chapter 8. For help in analyzing a specific job posting, consult your professors or career counselor.

A word about cover letters: When I conducted Exercise 14 in our senior seminar, most students found interesting job postings and picked out their meanings without much help. However, most wrote poor cover letters. Maybe you should take a look at *Killer Cover Letters* after all! This genre of writing is one you've had little experience with, so get help.

QUESTIONS YOU MIGHT BE ASKED IN AN INTERVIEW

There are many published lists of questions you are likely to be asked at some point in conversation with your future employer, so you should give them some thought now.

"Conversation?" you ask, "What about the formal interview, with the employer at her desk and my dossier open in front of her?"

Sociolinguistically speaking, the only difference between a conversation and an interview, in many cases, is intent. Many employers are as uncomfortable with a formal interview as you are, so they try to make it as American and informal as they can—walking in the hall, touring the labs, and so on. But *still they're trying to decide about you.* Anything you say and do in any interaction with this person may be observed and evaluated.

Questions you will be asked fall into about four categories: (1) your education, (2) your match with the organization, (3) your career goals, and (4) your personality and character. These are sincere questions that deserve good answers. So that you can begin preparing your answers, I've assembled some into Exercise 12, "Interviewing Yourself," at the back of this workbook.

There are also published lists of questions that employers are *not* allowed to ask you, and your career services can advise you about how to parry them. Here are some examples that are perhaps sincerely intended but are definitely illegal:

- Do you plan to get married (or have children)?
- Have you ever been treated for any of the following diseases . . . ?
- To what clubs and associations do you belong?

- What is your father's nationality?
- Have you ever been arrested? (It is legal, however, to ask whether you have been convicted.)

Don't forget to hold up your end of the conversation, with good questions, observations, and indications that you know yourself and the organization. Prepare carefully in advance and carry a few notes to prompt you.

Exercise 10, "Organizational Analysis," and Exercise 13, "Building Rapport with a Potential Employer," can help you win an offer.

Exercises

These exercises are linked to specific sections of the workbook, but they can be conducted whenever you need them. The exercises are not just to be read. They're like recipes: if you want to eat, then cook.

Ethnosemantics

In this exercise you will discover through ethnographic field methods what *other* people think anthropology is, how they think it relates to occupations, to the world today, to other social sciences, and to the natural sciences. The better you grasp the cultural meaning of *anthropology,* the better you can use or challenge that meaning.

One of the tasks of ethnosemantics is to diagram how a speaking community sorts and labels groups of related words. The cultural theory behind this task is that the way speakers think about a thing is mediated—and thereby shaped—by their language for that thing.

For example, I ask my students to sort a group of animal names into categories. My list includes *starfish, cockroach, clam,* and *wasp,* among others. A few of the students sort these words into the same categories that biologists use: *arthropods, echinoderms, bivalves,* and so on. Many students, however, sort them in two other ways. Many sort by the creature's habitat, such as "lives in the sea" and "lives on land." Most sort these words into categories such as "dangerous" or "edible."

The above exercise, I claim, shows that speakers of English will first think of these animals anthropocentrically (i.e., their relevance to humans), secondarily they think of animals ecologically, and finally they may pay attention to anatomical structure.

How do people think of anthropology? The answer to that question influences how they'll react when you mention it or write it on your résumé.

PROCEDURE

Write the following terms on index cards in large block letters. Put one term on each card.

Anthropologist	Geographer
Economist	Historian
Sociologist	Political scientist
Psychologist	Geologist

Conduct the following survey with several people. Tell your informant, "I'm trying to learn how people think of these words. This is not a test, just a method for learning what people share in their thinking. Here are eight occupations. Sort them into fewer than eight piles, based on whatever criteria you consider important."

When the sorting is done, note which cards are in which piles. Ask your informant to explain the category for each pile. The answer might be along the lines of "These are the ones I'd like to be," or "These are the most employable ones," or "This group uses scientific methods." Ask why anthropology was put in *this* pile instead of *that* pile, and note the reason given.

You might ask some follow-up questions, such as "What's the difference between *anthropologist* and *sociologist*?" or "What words come to mind when you think of *anthropologist*?"

To analyze the responses, identify the words that express the criteria that each informant used to distinguish among the categories. Are there similarities among your informants in their criteria? Note especially the position of anthropologist among the other professionals. Draw a chart like the one below to present your data, using the criteria shared among your informants instead of the categories I used ("highly paid," "exciting," etc.). Conclude by predicting how people like your informants would respond to anthropologists if they thought of them as they reported, and determine how you should renegotiate that response.

Americans' Classification of Some Professions (A Mock Chart)

	Works in business world		Works in academia	
	Highly paid	Not	**Exciting**	Not
Scientific	Economist Geologist		Geographer	Psychologist
Social	Political scientist	Sociologist	*Anthropologist*	Historian

A Literature Survey

Before going into the field to conduct research, the anthropologist surveys the literature to acquire an overview of what's been done and by whom. That knowledge will influence what to study in the field and what methods to use, and the anthropologist will refer to that literature when reporting the research. Similarly, before you apply for graduate school or for a job, you can do some homework to get a sense of current trends in your field. You will mention these when applying to graduate school, writing research grants, or courting an employer, thus demonstrating that you're aware of what's happening around you.

THE DISCIPLINARY LITERATURE

If you are interested in anthropology as a profession and want to teach, then *Anthropology News* is important. Borrow the last ten issues (it's not published in July or August) and browse through them in chronological order. A few of the recurring topics lately have included ethics in the field, how to promote anthropology to American decision makers, and the anthropological perspective on the global economy. Some other questions to answer during your browsing:

1. Which schools have scholars who are doing interesting work?

2. What kinds of books and research are winning prizes?

3. Which subdisciplines have the most interesting columns?

4. What kinds of work are being conducted by those who send queries to the "Cooperation Column"?

5. Look at the list of grants funded by the National Science Foundation (NSF). Many of these are for doctoral students. NSF grants are usually for the more "scientific" and "pure" research projects: a large proportion are archaeology, primatology, and genetics. The National Endowment for the Humanities (NEH) supports research that is more humanistic. The Ford Foundation supports projects that might help reduce a world problem, such as hunger or ethnic conflict. The Wenner Gren Foundation also supports much anthropological research. What research topics gain support?

6. Does AAA or its affiliates sell any publications that might be useful to you?

If you are interested in graduate training in anthropology and related fields but seek a nonacademic career, you can pose a similar set of questions to *Practicing Anthropology,* a bimonthly magazine published by the Society for Applied Anthropology.

CAREER LITERATURE

Besides the disciplinary literature, written by anthropologists but with many other purposes besides career advice, there is the career-oriented literature, which has a good overview on career development today, although it may not say much about anthropology in particular. Your career services library or college library will have some of this career literature.

Select a career field and investigate the relevant literature on your campus. I have selected travel and tourism because several years ago one of my advisees went into that field. I find my career services library has five items in that field:

1. *Opportunities in Travel Careers*
2. *The Official Guide to Travel Agent and Travel Careers*
3. *Travel and Hospitality Career Directory*
4. *Travel and Tourism Careers Guide Book*
5. *Career Opportunities in Tourism and the Hospitality Industry*

Note who published the guide. If it is an occupational association (such as the National Association of Forensic Sciences), then write for a list of its career-oriented publications. Write a summary of the most interesting things you learn from this review. Some points to cover:

1. Where is the work?

2. Who does one work for?

3. What are the tasks like?

4. What skills and personal qualities will a successful professional in this field need?

5. What training is needed for entry or promotion within the field?

6. How can you relate your training in anthropology to this field?

**Examples of Useful References in
My College's Careers Services Library**

(What's in *Yours?*)

Directory of Internships, Work Experience Programs, and On the Job Training Opportunities

The Complete Guide to Environmental Careers

Great Careers: Guide to Careers, Internships, and Volunteer Opportunities in the Nonprofit Sector

New Career Opportunities in Health and Human Services

Museum Careers, from *Museum News*

Good Works: A Guide to Social Change Careers

Research Centers Directory

U.S. Forest Service Volunteer Opportunities. Internships

Opportunities in Human Resources Management (Personnel) Careers

Liberal Arts Jobs (job descriptions; includes skills inventory and how to interview professionals in the field to see whether the job fits you)

Opportunities in Social Work Careers

Participant Observation

The goal of participant observation is to learn what it is to be an x doing y, and the method is to hang around with xs who are actually doing y so that you can watch, ask questions, and learn by trial and error how to do y yourself.

This exercise helps you to understand what it is to be an anthropologist (in Part 1) or some other occupation (Part 1).

PART 1: ATTENDING AN ANTHROPOLOGY CONFERENCE

Almost every semester there will be some professional get-together within a day's drive of you. Annual conferences are held by state or regional associations, or special subdisciplines of anthropologists, like historic archaeologists, primatologists, or applied anthropologists. The calendar in the back of the *Anthropology News* will list some. If your professors are alerted to your interest, they can pass to you the flyers they receive almost weekly in the mail. There is usually a reduced registration fee for students, and inexpensive lodging can be arranged.

Like the Inupiat people of Canada's far north, the anthropological tribe comes together in the fall to share resources, exchange news, look over each other's latest productions, dance and play, barter goods, adjudicate disputes, establish cooperative hunting and trade partnerships, and conduct a few group rituals. You will note that some of this takes place in formal settings at announced times, whereas some of this occurs impromptu in hallways.

You'll want to enlist a few key informants—professors or students—to explain what you are seeing. To learn more about research that interests you, speak informally with a paper presenter at the conclusion of the session.

Because everyone wears name tags indicating school or organizational affiliation, ask professors or graduate students about their graduate school programs, or ask a practicing anthropologist about the nature of his or her work with the Brooklyn Zoo (or wherever).

Ideally, you would yourself propose and deliver a report at the conference, which greatly improves your entrée because then you are seen as "one of us."

PART 2: SHADOWING

Shadowing means following your informant around for a day or so while he or she works. Not only will you pick up a feel for the pace, interactions, and tasks the informant performs, but many opportunities will arise for talking about the job, too. While shadowing your informant, you will meet others with whom you can talk later.

Your purpose is to learn about the job, not to get hired right now. You must make that clear in order to set your informant and the organization at ease. There is no question, however, that if the shadowing leaves a good impression, the organization will look more favorably on an application from you later.

The following procedure works. You may shorten it if you already know your contact well enough to arrange the preliminary interview informally. But informal does not mean casual; following these steps is a courtesy and shows that you have social expertise.

Selecting the Person to Shadow

The informant should have the authority to make an appointment with you, have enough experience in the field to be a good informant, and be senior enough to know other people in responsible positions in the organization, or in other organizations, to whom you can be referred.

Write Before You Call

Introduce yourself and your interests and request a meeting to talk with your informant about the field. Present yourself as one who is trying to learn more for your career planning, not trying to get a job offer. Say that you'll call.

Call for an Appointment

About two weeks after the letter is sent, call your informant-to-be to request a meeting. Remind her or him of the letter you sent, emphasize your desire to develop your long-range career plans, and request about an hour to explore some questions you have. Say that an hour of time would be ideal but you'll be glad to have whatever time he or she can give. Occasionally, the potential informant is reluctant because your call comes at a bad time for the organization, or he or she is too new to the job to have a perspective yet. If you encounter hesitancy, assure the person that this is not a pressing matter and propose to call back in several weeks.

The Preliminary Interview

Like the ethnographer in another culture, you don't know much about how things really work here, but you've done some homework and you're well trained to find out more, efficiently and with a modicum of grace. Ask questions that reveal your interests and abilities. For example, don't ask a global question such as "What does a person do in this career?" Instead, ask, "How much [grant writing or computer work or speaking Spanish] might a person do in this work?" or "How much do you work in a team versus independently?"

Request Referrals

Build your research network: ask whether there is someone else in the organization, or in another organization, whose work might also clarify your plans. Conclude your appointment a few minutes early to show that you are aware of time and consider your informant a busy person.

Ask to Shadow

If you have the right informant and you seem to be getting along, then at the conclusion of your appointment, say the following:

> It would be a great help to me if I could observe the career in action for, say, a day. This is called "shadowing." It would be ideal if we could arrange a time soon when I could shadow you for a day. Would that be possible?

If this is not possible, be gracious and understanding, ask to be introduced to one of the referrals, and start the process over again with a request for appointment, a phone call, and a preliminary interview. If shadowing is possible with your first informant, try to settle on a specific date, follow up with a thank-you note and a confirmation letter, and phone your informant close to the date to confirm it.

Participant Observation

The guidelines are simple:

> Be all eyes and ears.
> Take few notes except when alone.
> Treat all others you come in contact with as future informants.
> Ask questions whenever you are given cues that questions are
>   acceptable.

Features to watch for:

> Tasks performed
> Work settings
> Skills required
> Persons the informant interacts with
> Pace and atmosphere

Debrief yourself thoroughly in writing after you've left.

Follow Up

Send a letter within a week expressing gratitude and a desire to keep the communication open.

EXERCISE 4

Demography

Most fieldwork eventually requires some careful analysis of the population under study. How many of these people are there? What is the gender and age composition? How has the population been changing? To acquire an overview of the anthropological profession—at least that portion of it in universities and research institutes—you may conduct a demographic analysis of the *AAA Guide to Departments of Anthropology*. Most anthropology departments purchase this publication; it is one of the essential directories of the profession and a very handy advising tool.

Examine the sections at the back of the book titled "Sources of Degrees . . ." and "Degrees Granted." Which ten schools are producing the most Ph.D.s and M.A.s? Consult the section titled "Degrees Held by Individuals Listed . . ." What level of degree is held by staff members in museums, research institutes, libraries, or labs? Last, consult the section titled "Ph.D. Dissertations . . ." What topics are graduate students working on these days? From analysis of these titles, you may learn where students are doing work like you want to do.

From the central section of the guide, define a sample of fifteen universities that interest you. List the gender and year of degree of the faculty at those schools. Aim for a sample of about a hundred individuals. (Note: Year of degree is here used as a shortcut to age of individual; however, because many Ph.D. holders receive their degree many years after completing college, this number will overstate the youth of the population.)

Gender	Year of Degree
M	1967
F	1980
. . .	. . .

107

Next, construct a population pyramid by sorting the above list into the following categories:

Degree	Male	Female
Before 1965 (e.g.)	3	1
1966–70	2	2
1971–75	10	5
1976–80		
1981–85		
1986–90		
1991–95		
1996–		

Examine the size of the left- and right-hand sides of this chart over this time period. What has been the change in gender participation in the teaching profession in your sample?

For ease in visualizing the data, construct a population pyramid (Figure E.1). Examine the shape of the pyramid, from apex (the older professionals) to base (the younger professionals). Has the population of academic anthropologists been engaging in replacement—that is, adding new recruits in recent years? Will the population be stable for a while or will it experience a lot of turnover about the time you complete your Ph.D. (eight years from

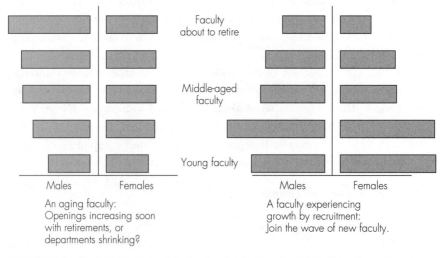

FIGURE E.1   Population Pyramids for Academic Faculty, 2000: Two Scenarios

now, if you are a senior)? If the population pyramid is truly pyramidal, meaning wide at the base of recent anthropologists and tapering at the apex of elder anthropologists, then recruitment has been heavy. If the pyramid has vertical sides or is wide at the top, then there is a cohort of older anthropologists who will leave the profession soon. After all, someone who completed a Ph.D. in 1970 at twenty-eight years old has been thinking seriously about retirement during the last couple of years. If you see an upside-down pyramid, then the population is very elderly and has recruited very few new members lately.

Besides teaching you an anthropological method, this analysis has practical value to you. It provides clues to your opportunities for academic employment years down the road when you enter the academic job market.

Transcultural Self-Presentation: The Résumé

To repeat what I said in Chapter 1, explaining yourself as an anthropology major to a potential employer is very similar to explaining yourself to hosts and informants when beginning fieldwork. Both situations boil down to tests of your transcultural communication skill: knowing their world, knowing your own, and then making a convincing translation that increases their respect for and trust of you.

This exercise helps you translate your anthropological abilities and experiences into language that is attractive and intelligible to employers who do not know anthropology—which is most of them.

Workshops offered at your college and manuals available at your bookstore can help you translate what you have thought of as ordinary life experiences into attractive résumé items showing that you will make a good employee. In this exercise you will focus on translating your anthropological experiences (or desired *future* anthropological experiences, if you haven't had many yet) into job-related terms.

First, take a holistic view of résumés as cultural texts. In little more than a page, a résumé provokes interest in you as a person who can do—or *learn* to do—what an employer wants. Your past is of little interest except as it suggests what you will do in the position you're applying for. So present your experiences as examples of the actions you can perform and the skills you can utilize.

Even college classes can reveal those actions and skills. For example, my student Grebbleberry got a B in my cultural ecology class, during which she wrote and presented a term paper on the effects of deforestation on Amazonian indigenous peoples. Stated in those terms, no employer is going to sit up and pay attention.

But if we say that Grebbleberry "demonstrated good ability to analyze human–environmental interrelationships, to conduct independent library research, to write a word-processed report under pressure of a deadline, and to make an oral presentation of research results," does she sound more employable now? If she can also claim that she has experience working in a team and had an excellent attendance record, she's golden.

Now it's your turn: in the left column of the following chart, list your anthropology coursework and related experiences (jobs, volunteering, clubs, awards, summer field schools). In the center column, identify the things that you did in that course (write synopses of complex texts, research current legislation, analyze television programs, etc.). In the right-hand column, translate these activities into the language that résumé readers would understand. Refer to the list of twelve abilities in Chapter 5 for appropriate words and phrases.

Anthropological Experiences	*Activities and Accomplishments*	*Résumé Language*

Social-Network Analysis

Analyze your own network: Where are your useful connections to someone who knows about work that interests you? For example, your next-door neighbor may have interesting work. Since you already know her, she is a first-order connection (see "you" and "Lil" in Figure E.2). Second-order connections are those millions of "friends of friends." For example, alumni who are doing interesting work can be met through your professors (see "you"-"Albert"-"Sarah" in the figure). Among these first- and second-order connections are dozens of people you should talk with, some of whom you might shadow to find out what their work is like (see Exercise 3). Others you might interview as potential employers (see Exercise 13).

Connection	First-Order	Second-Order
Neighbors	Johnny's mom: works in county museum	She may know director at Nevada State Museum.
Friends		
Employers		
Teachers		

Connection	*First-Order*	*Second-Order*
Coworkers		
Family		
Organizational (church, club)		
Fellow students		
Other		

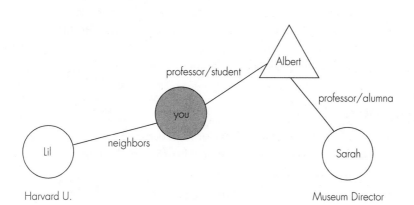

FIGURE E.2   First- and Second-Order Connections in Social Networks

Life History: A Recent Ph.D.

In this exercise, you will collect the life history of an anthropologist who received a Ph.D. in the last five years. You'll be trying to identify the pivotal decision points in this person's career. Your informant's experience may be of use to you as you think about graduate school.

A life-history interview is usually quite loosely structured; the informant talks, and you listen, interrupting now and then to ask a question for clarification. You carry only a list of topics that you want to be addressed. If the informant doesn't mention one of them, you ask to talk about it.

In current life-history methods, the informant is allowed to define the key terms and the key events of the story. You don't force the informant to follow a simple time line, for example, and you don't force the informant to confront your interpretation of the story. Your task is primarily to create good rapport between you, to place the two of you in a conducive environment for the storytelling, and to be a faithful recorder. Tape the story so you can capture the language and the tone. Later, when analyzing the life history, you'll not only present the informant's point of view but also ask questions of the story from your etic, or comparative, point of view.

PROCEDURE

1. Select a professor who earned her or his doctorate recently, or ask to be introduced to someone in the area who did so. Your informant might even still be writing the dissertation.

2. Arrange an interview during which you won't be interrupted for about half an hour.

3. Turn on the tape recorder and begin with some casual conversation to get you both used to the machine: ("I'm . . . and we're here to . . . Tell me your name . . . where did you earn your Ph.D. . . . when . . . what was

your subject of research . . ."). Maintain good eye contact and a conversational manner. Jot down only questions you want to ask.

4. To focus the interview, ask how your informant became interested in anthropology and how she or he got from that point to today. You are hoping that your informant will volunteer how she or he made pivotal career decisions. Here is a partial list:

Whether to major in anthropology

Whether and when to go to graduate school

Which graduate school to attend

Which professor (or professors) to study with

Where to do research and on what topic

Whether to pursue a postdoctoral position or look for a job

Where to look for a position

Why take this position

5. If the preceding topics don't arise in your informant's story, ask about them. For example, ". . . uh . . . before we talk about Indiana's graduate program, can you tell me how you decided to go to graduate school at all?"

6. Offer to give your informant a copy of your report. Invite her or him to append corrections and alternative interpretations to your report.

7. Listen again to the tape, jotting notes that are at least a fair summary of your informant's point of view, if not a literal transcription of what was said.

8. Write a summary of your informant's presentation of her or his professional biography.

9. Write a brief analysis of your informant's story. Which characteristics or aspects of his or her life (devotion to family, Hispanic heritage, skill at math, or desire to do applied work) appear repeatedly in your informant's explanations of decisions? How do the decisions compare to the ones you imagine you would make? Which of your informant's characteristics apply to you, and which others would you need to add?

Internetworking

Since I began composing this workbook in early 1995, the World Wide Web (WWW) has continued to grow exponentially, and the anthropology and career resources therein are now rich and numerous. Be warned, however: the Web is a kind of rapidly growing library lacking any acquisitions policy or quality standards. Anyone can publish anything. The burden is on you to sift the accurate information from the erroneous or intentionally deceiving.

This exercise introduces you to Web sites for graduate school, careers, research projects, and e-mail networking with other anthropologists and students. To conduct this exercise, you will connect to the WWW via a browsing application like Netscape on a desktop computer. If you are new to this, get a friend to help you. A few Web-surfing skills are needed to perform this exercise:

- Keep track of the sites you've visited so you can return to them. This tracking is usually done via a "Go" menu at the top of your screen that allows you to navigate back and forth among the sites you've visited during a session. Record the URLs (addresses) of the sites you might revisit in future sessions. A URL looks like this: *http://www.potsdam.edu/~lib.html.*

- Save pages of useful information as bookmarks or as files on your own computer so you may consult them at leisure.

- Learn to search the Web using key terms. For example, my browser offers a "Net Search" button in its toolbar that, when clicked, brings you to a variety of search tools and guides for how to use them. Whatever engine you use, I recommend studying the "help" and "options" features offered. A successful Web user must be a versatile searcher.

PROCEDURE

The goal of this exercise is to report on examples of sites listed on the following page. Here are some suggested search strategies.

1.   Connect to the World Wide Web by opening your browsing application. Go to the searching tools and search for the key word *anthropology, archaeology* (and *archeology*), *linguistics,* or *forensic.*

The search will generate a list of hundreds of Web sites related to anthropology (or your search term). It will display the site titles about a dozen at a time. Scan the display, call for the next dozen and scan them, then call for the next dozen or go back to the first dozen, until you have a sense of the variety available to you.

Notice that the list is a mixed bag of universities, libraries, research institutes, publications, personal home pages, and commercial sites. Any term underlined is "clickable" and brings that site to you.

Explore underlined items on the list by clicking on them, following any new links you find intriguing. When you reach a dead end, go back until you are back on track and branch off in a new direction. You can always return to your list of search results by selecting it from the Go menu at the top of your screen.

2.   Search for the key word *careers* or, in the search options, search for the co-occurence of *career* and *anthropology* and follow the same procedures as above.

3.   Visit your college's career services home page and branch out from there. If your college doesn't have a site, try my college's at *http://www. potsdam.edu/career/internetCareers.html.*

4.   A fine general-purpose careers Web site is Jobweb, at *http://www. jobweb.org/catapult/catapult.htm.*

Resource	*Site Address (URL)*	*Notes about Contents*
1. A guide to writing résumés		

Resource	*Site Address (URL)*	*Notes about Contents*
2. Opportunities for fieldwork and training		
3. Programs for study abroad		
4. Title and author of an article in an on-line journal		
5. A graduate school program that appeals to you		
6. Graphics of hominid fossils		

Resource	Site Address (URL)	Notes about Contents
7. Career advice on archaeology, linguistics, or physical anthropology		
8. The home page of a graduate student or researcher at an institution that interests you		
9. The e-mail address and description of a discussion group in anthropology		
10. Something else that appears useful about anthropology or careers but is not listed above		

Analysis of Survey Data

The box on pages 121–124 provides unsorted data from my own department's alumni survey, which I invite you to analyze. Here's one way to do that: Create a tabulation sheet with seventeen rows and four columns. The names of the rows are the seventeen categories that Kratts and Hunter used in their survey reported in Table 7.1. The names of the columns are "1970s," "1980s," and "1990s." Split each of those three columns into two and label one Male and one Female. Now you have a table with 102 boxes, as in the following:

Occupation	1970s		1980s		1990s	
	Male	Female	Male	Female	Male	Female
Management						
Student						
Teacher or Professor						
etc.						

Assign each individual in the box on pages 121–124 to one of the boxes of your tabulation sheet. Make a tick mark in that box. When all individuals are tabulated, count up and record the number of marks in each box. Now look for patterns in the data. You can check, for example, whether there is a difference in the work that men and women do and how the current occupations of the older alumni differ from the occupations of the recent alumni.

Current Occupations of SUNY Potsdam Anthropology B.A. Alumni

Sales representative, florist (f, '92)

Comanager, shop (f, '92)

Graduate student, public health school (f, '92)

Graduate student, museum studies (f, '92)

Graduate student, counseling school (m, '92)

Sales representative, electronics store (m, '92)

Substitute teacher, public school (m, '92)

Cashier, grocery store (f, '92)

Passenger service assistant, airline (f, '92)

Operations clerk, fuel company (f, '92)

Nurse administrator, psychiatric center (f, '92)

Archivist/registrar, county museum (f, '92)

Case examiner, social work (f, '83)

Residence counselor, home for disabled (f, '90)

Assistant customer service manager, grocery store (f, '88)

Manager, corporation (f, '87)

Dentist, private practice (f, '78)

Agent, insurance corporation (m, '81)

Professional musician, self-employed (m, '86)

Intelligence analyst, U.S. Army (m, '87)

Audiovisual coordinator, public school (f, '75)

General manager, scuba shop (m, '74)

Marketing assistant, insurance broker (f, '82)

General contractor, self-employed (m, '75)

Sales manager, broadcasting corporation (f, '71)

Teacher, private school (m, '72)

Teacher, Catholic school (f, '72)

Lawyer, private practice (m, '75)

Credit and collections agent, financial company (f, '80)

(continued)

Current Occupations of SUNY Potsdam
Anthropology B.A. Alumni *(continued)*

Financial analyst, brokerage firm (m, '73)

Teacher, history, public school (f, '79)

Paralegal worker, law firm (f, '82)

Principal, public school (f, '72)

Acting supervisor, post office (f, '71)

Social worker, town board of education (f, '75)

Manager and owner, gift shop (f, '74)

Forklift operator, manufacturer (m, '79)

Teacher, public school (f, '71)

Principal, public school (m, '71)

Customer service representative, store (f, '79)

Environmental analyst, New York State Department
of Environmental Conservation (m, '74)

Officer, U.S. Marines (m, '91)

Parole agent, State of Colorado (m, '71)

Graduate student, university (f, '89)

Quality control technician, manufacturing (f, '79)

Graduate student, university (m, '75)

Probation supervisor, county (m, '74)

Department manager and senior scientist, manufacturing (m, '79)

Medical oncology nurse, hospital (f, '79)

Financial administrator, UNICEF (f, '88)

Sales representative, jewelry manufacturing (m, '79)

Social worker, consulting firm (f, '84)

Counselor, community college (f, '91)

Staff sonographer, hospital (m, '79)

Research archaeologist, university (f, '74)

Teacher, public school (f, '83)

Key operator, technical services company (m, '90)

Head welfare examiner, county government (m, '72)

Graduate student, anthropology (f, '88)

Education coordinator, children's museum (f, '84)

Library technician, library (f, '85)

Teacher, elementary school (f, '80)

Teacher, child care center (f, '89)

Social work assistant, school for mentally retarded (f, '76)

Senior associate engineer, manufacturing (m, '76)

Assistant director of alumni affairs, university (f, '86)

Teacher, elementary school (f, '89)

Public service assistant, university (f, '82)

Sales representative, manufacturing (f, '79)

Field archaeologist, consulting firm (f, '87)

Owner, management consulting firm (m, '82)

Nurse, mental health center (f, '82)

Director of counseling, college (f, '81)

Assistant coach, university (m, '90)

Account manager, data services company (f, '82)

Owner, motel (m, '81)·

Archaeologist, Smithsonian (f, '84)

Accounts manager, communications company (f, '79)

Teacher of gifted, public school (f, '71)

Senior parole officer, New York State Division of Parole (m, '75)

Customer service agent, telephone company (m, '85)

Health care coordinator, county home (m, '80)

Security specialist, U.S. Army (f, '77)

Probation officer, county government (m, '74)

Teacher, elementary school (f, '88)

Teacher, Native American school (m, '75)

Archaeological fieldworker, state government (f, '89)

Office manager, county government (f, '77)

Research technician, county government (f, '72)

Teacher, state department of labor job corps (f, '71)

Case analyst, Veteran's Administration (m, '69)

Owner, wedding shop (f, '80)   *(continued)*

Current Occupations of SUNY Potsdam Anthropology B.A. Alumni *(continued)*

Nurse administrator, psychiatric center (m, '80)

Publications associate, university (f, '85)

Senior planner, manufacturing corporation (f, '73)

Media services coordinator, County Board of Cooperative Educational Services (f, '71)

Teacher, reading (f, '69)

Student, chiropractic school (m, '85)

Clerk, bookstore (f, '83)

Teacher, remedial reading, public school (f, '75)

Associate professor of anthropology, university (f, '72)

Postmaster, post office (f, '80)

Grants manager, Native American tribal council (m, '83)

Teacher, public school (f, '74)

Principal, arts school (m, '72)

Graduate student, university (f, '87)

Tax compliance representative, state tax department (m, '81)

Archaeologist and lab director, consulting firm (f, '77)

Family counseling director, human services center (m, '72)

Staffer, Central America lobbying group (f, '84)

Social worker, special children's center (f, '76)

Buyer, commercial press (m, '86)

Freelance illustrator, technical drawings (f, '77)

Project director, private community research firm (f, '78)

Marketing consultant, international management consulting firm (m, '82)

Library services coordinator, County BOCES (f, '71)

Quality assurance supervisor, optician shop chain (f, '77)

Source: Office of Alumni Affairs, SUNY College at Potsdam. Used with permission.

Organizational Analysis

In this exercise you will discover the workings of some professional organization in anthropology or in an occupational category that interests you. Knowing how an organization functions increases the effectiveness of your networking by helping you to meet the right people, learn useful facts, behave in the appropriate way, and find a niche for yourself. As I point out repeatedly in this workbook, good career development is like good fieldwork. Formal organizational analysis is a valuable method both for the ethnographic fieldworker and for the new college graduate in the job market.

PROCEDURE

Select a subgroup of anthropologists, such as the Society for Urban Anthropology or the Massachusetts Archaeological Society, or some interdisciplinary group, like the Social Science Task Force on AIDS, or some occupational group that interests you, like the American Association of Chiropractors. Your college's department of anthropology can also serve as the subject of this exercise; for students interested in academic anthropology, studying a department will exemplify how life is lived in the local lineage of the professional tribe.

The best research method is to *triangulate,* which means to collect information about the same topic from two or more sources, which either corroborate each other or reveal the difference between the real and the ideal. For type 1 data, select an informant who is a member of that organization; for type 2 data, collect some literature from the group, which you can borrow from your informant or request in writing; for type 3 data, watch the organization in action. Even if only one or two of these sources are available, a useful picture can emerge.

A formal organizational analysis answers the following questions:

1. What is the group's charter, or statement of purpose? Is it written, perhaps as a constitution and bylaws, or is it strictly an oral tradition?

2. According to that charter, what are the functions of the group?

3. How are members recruited, initiated, enculturated, and rewarded?

4. What are the rights and responsibilities of a member of the group?

5. What are the titles and responsibilities of the special roles, such as the officers?

6. Is there a status hierarchy in the group? What defines it?

7. What rituals does the group perform to maintain solidarity, identity, authority, or legitimacy?

8. How are decisions made?

9. When and how do members get together or interact?

10. Does the group communally own any valuable assets or special paraphernalia?

11. What are the sanctions for deviant behavior? What degree of control does the group have over its members?

Working with Key Informants

The following questions can be asked of a professor one at a time, every time you two meet at the water fountain. You get fairly short answers that way, but the interview is recursive: you return to the topic again and again, which gives your informant the greatest opportunity to remember something useful since the last time you spoke. Or you can arrange for a few minutes to talk with him or her in a quiet concentrated way. In either case, take a few notes and thoroughly debrief yourself later. Listening and remembering are high arts in ethnography!

LEVEL 1: FOR THE NEW ANTHROPOLOGY STUDENT

The purpose of this interview segment is to enlist your professor as a key informant to visualize anthropology as a career and a set of skills rather than something to study in a textbook.

1. How did you get interested in anthropology?

2. What did your parents and friends think when you got into anthropology?

3. How do you explain anthropology to other people?

4. Have you ever worked—or do you now work—at anything other than teaching?

5. What sort of research or public service do you do? What anthropological skills do you use in that work?

6. Describe for me what goes on in [a course that your informant teaches that interests you].

7. Can you show me your lab (or other examples of your work)?

8. Question of your choice:

9. Question of your choice:

LEVEL 2: FOR THE ADVANCED ANTHROPOLOGY STUDENT

The purpose of this interview segment is to engage your professor as a key informant to help you expand your network and gain entrée into useful places. It is assumed that you've developed some interests in the field by now, such as forensics or contract archaeology or AIDS research.

1. Who has graduated from [this department] who is interested in the same things I am?

2. Who has a job like the one I'd like to have?

3. Is there an organization or newsletter for people interested in these things?

4. Where should I go to graduate school if I am interested in this type of work?

5. Is there a school or organization near here where work like this is being done?

6. Do you know anyone at that school or organization?

7. Do you receive any journals or newsletters that might deal with the work that interests me?

8. Are there any workshops or conferences or other professional get-togethers coming up on this topic, and can you help me to attend?

9. Question of your choice:

10. Question of your choice:

Interviewing Yourself

Soon, in an important conversation, a potential employer is going to ask you questions like the ones posed here, so now is a good time to give them some thought. Similar kinds of self-knowledge are often expected in the "personal essay" you are asked to include in your application to graduate school. Imagine a graduate program or employment situation you would like to aim for. The boss (or the professor) is walking down the hall with you, giving you a tour of the facilities but asking a lot of questions, too. Sketch out a first draft of what you say in response.

1. About your education

   Why did you choose to major in anthropology?

2. About your match with the organization

   In what ways do you think you can make a contribution to our organization?

Why are you interested in working for (or studying at) our organization (or school)?

3. About your career goals

   What do you see yourself doing five years from now?

   What is it that interests you about this occupation or field of study?

4. About your personality and character

   Which of your recent accomplishments have given you the most satisfaction? Why?

   Describe a recent incident when you had to stand your ground on something you felt strongly about.

Building Rapport with a Potential Employer

Learning the culture of employers and the rules of the hiring game may actually be undertaken as a research project. After all, who better than the Smithsonian could advise you on a career in museums; who better than WNEW could advise you on a career in broadcast media? My college's office of career services proposes a set of five steps for gaining entrée and collecting useful information, not to mention increasing rapport.

1. *Begin with a literature search* as all fieldworkers do. Examine both secondary sources (there are compendia that describe organizations) and primary sources (literature from the organization you want to work for). By this literature search or through your networks you identify the person in the organization whom you want to be your key informant. In most cases, this will be the person who would supervise you. Your goal is for that key informant and you to get to know one another.

2. *Contact the organization directly* to identify your key informant. Career services can offer tips for getting past the *gatekeepers*—the receptionists and applicant interviewers whose job it is to screen their bosses from you.

3. *Write to your key informant* to arrange a telephone conversation. Follow up the letter by telephoning to arrange an interview. The interview is not simply for a job because the organization may be in window 1, where not everyone is certain they are going to hire soon. The reason for the interview is to learn about the organization and to seek your key informant's advice in career planning.

4. *Conduct the interview* in a conversational style. This interview is only somewhat structured, which means that you bring a set of topics you'd like to hear addressed before you gratefully depart. As the ethnographer, you take the lead, asking questions and telling enough about yourself that you can request advice. Do not use a tape recorder or clipboard; just use a small pad to jot specific details or keep a list of topics. Debriefing yourself immediately after the talk will catch most of it.

5. *Follow up soon* with a thank-you letter. If you liked the organization, tell them so and express a desire to work for them should a vacancy occur. Even if you never get a job with them, you've learned about the career from the experts and made some more network contacts. It is not uncommon for your key informant to tip you off about opportunities in the making with other organizations.

Interpreting the Text

Chapter 9 introduced the job ad as a text requiring close reading and nego-tiation. In this exercise you'll study some examples of annotated job an-nouncements; then you'll collect your own and analyze them. The outcome may be either a cover letter, if you are ready for the position, or a plan for self-improvement during your remaining college years.

Here's a description of a federal internship opportunity posted on the Internet, with my annotations.

Indian Programs Assistant
Environmental Protection Agency,
Office of Solid Waste,
Washington, D.C.

The assistant will work with the National Native American Program manager in the Office of Solid Waste (OSW) on a variety of tasks and activities associated with implementing the Resource Conservation and Recovery Act (RCRA) on Indian lands.

◄ *Any course work or volunteer work related to solid waste or Native American studies?*

◄ *Research the agency and read about the RCRA.*

These tasks will include, but are not lim-ited to

• Production of the *Native American Network*, a national newsletter for tribes, and other technical information publications

◄ *Here's room for you to promote your other abilities, such as Web page design, experience on the school newspaper, tech-nical writing course.*

• Monitoring the Tribal Lands Military Munitions Rule Outreach and Consultation project

◄ *Do you have any military experience?*

• Developing a national tribal hazardous waste strategy and grant program

◄ *Work on college committees usually involves strategy. Have you taken any environmental studies courses?*

• Monitoring of OSW tribal program grants, such as the Solid Waste Circuit Rider program

◄ *A good reason to get grant-writing and management experience early*

- Coordinating and drafting program briefings

◄ A familiar synthesis task for you

- Drafting correspondence

- Preliminary planning for the 2000 National Tribal Conference on Environmental Management

◄ Have you helped with a conference before?

The assistant will be exposed to national program activities and gain an understanding of tribal waste-management issues related to legislation, regulations, policies, and guidance. Limited travel to various Indian reservations may be available.

◄ An enticement but not certain

Qualifications: B.A./B.S. degree. Must have excellent verbal, written, organizational, and teamwork skills. Must be adaptable to perform a wide variety of tasks. Experience working with Indian tribal government is preferred.

◄ Favors Native American candidates. Lacking this, perhaps you have studied or visited a reservation community.

Terms: Full-time, 26 weeks, up to $12.50 per hour.

◄ The salary is low and the position temporary, but this is a foot in the door to permanent federal employment.

The following position, advertised in a metropolitan newspaper, might suit an applicant with a physical anthropology B.A. interested in animal behavior and active in university organizations. (I've changed the name of the employer.)

Coordinator, Zoo Volunteers
Acme City Zoo

Seeking experienced volunteer coordinator for the Acme City Zoo, a facility of a large conservation organization. The zoo's volunteer program has 100 active volunteer wildlife guides.

◄ Experience coordinating volunteers may have been at college rather than at a zoo. Zoo experience is a bonus.

Most desirable candidate will have experience supervising volunteers in a cultural institution, an academic background in the life sciences, and will have experience in producing educational programming. Responsibilities will include organizing and conducting a 10-week training course, coaching volunteers on the job, designing new educational programs for the zoo visitor, and developing a recruitment plan to expand the program.

◄ You can make a good case here; they didn't insist on a zoology degree.

◄ Opportunities for experience are frequent in college. At my college, residence hall assistants, teaching assistants, and some clubs do this.

◄ Have you helped supervise a dig or a lab?

Candidate must be able to work some weekends, holidays, and rotate days off in order to interact with all of the volunteers. The dynamic educator filling this position will have strong interpersonal and organi-

◄ An erratic schedule like this favors the unattached new B.A. holder. After four years of student life, you know erratic.

◄ Key on this critical sentence. What can you demonstrate from your previous employment or campus responsibilities? Education credentials would be valuable.

zational skills. Benefits include 3 weeks of vacation, medical/dental and life insurance, pension/401k.

◀ *Pretty good benefits. This has long-term potential if the salary is adequate for urban costs of living.*

This next position sounds like an excellent entrée into the National Park Service, for B.A.s or midcourse M.A.s. (I've abridged it slightly.)

Intern

National Park Service, Northeast Ethnography Program, Boston

The Student Conservation Association and the National Park Service are co-operating to offer a one-year internship described below:

The Northeast Ethnography Program develops, manages, and conducts research and technical-assistance projects that help more than 75 national parks to work effectively with diverse populations. Duties include implementing regional Ethnographic Resources Inventory; conducting archival and ethnographic research; developing project proposals and specifications; providing general program support, preparing briefings and reports for senior management; reviewing policy, regulatory, and research documents.

◀ *Experience in archaeological resources inventory can be parallel preparation.*

◀ *Skill in research papers and training in fieldwork can be offered here.*
◀ *Familiar ground for the good research paper writer.*

Position involves extensive use of qualitative databases, research materials and methods, tact and diplomacy in working with culturally diverse constitutents, park managers, and staff specialists on complex, frequently controversial issues. Training provided in ERI software, federal statutes, and NPS standards.

◀ *Ethnography students can show some familiarity with handling structured data.*
◀ *Any experience in a multicultural collaboration or campus politics?*

Require: B.A. in a social science discipline; strong computer, written, and oral communication skills; knowledge of or interest in working with American Indians, African Americans, or other cultural groups in the northeastern U.S.; ability to work independently; willingness to work in an office environment and travel, as needed. Desire: some graduate work in applied anthropology, public history, or a related field; ethnographic or ethnohistorical research experience.

◀ *Show them your database skills and speaking experience.*

◀ *Course work, term papers, organizations, and your own cultural background will go here.*

◀ *Some undergraduate programs offer as much training in this as do M.A. programs.*

This is a 12-month, full-time position. Compensation consists of travel costs to and from Big City, a weekly stipend, and monthly housing allowance. Members of groups that are historically underrepresented in the National Park Service are strongly encouraged to apply.

◄ Ideally, they'd like to hire a person of color, but the outcome still depends on the qualifications of those who apply, especially if you can supply some of the items in their "desire" list.

Now collect three position announcements that interest you. Internet discussion groups, professional newsletters, Web sites, and newspapers are good sources.

- Interpret them as I have done: identify the training and abilities they call for, pinpoint the key words, translate what they say into what they probably mean, and distinguish the required from the desired. Match up your abilities and experiences with these items.

- Identify areas that you want to negotiate—either you have abilities or experience that you think they need, or they have a need that you could meet in another way.

- If you are a graduating student, write the cover letter matching you up (as you hope to be at graduation) and making your negotiating points. If you still have a year or more before you take this job, identify what you need to do in the meantime to become qualified.

Know Thyself:
A Triangulation Using
Formal Interview Data

The two elements of a good career choice are knowing about the position and knowing about yourself. Both elements are improved by efforts you can make now. You can learn about the position through Exercises 7, 11, and 13. You can learn about yourself through Exercises 5, 12, and this one.

In this exercise you will conduct a structured, or formal, interview with yourself about yourself. Because you're a fallible informant, you'll corroborate (confirm) your answers by asking the same questions about you of a second, and perhaps even a third, person. We fieldworkers call this *triangulating* (see Figure E.3). When surveying to draw a map the archaeologist takes a sighting on the temple from two different locations to pinpoint more precisely its location. So too the ethnographer homes in on the truth

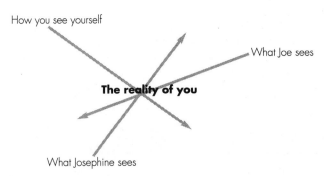

FIGURE E.3   Triangulation

about something by asking more than one person and noting where their answers   converge.

Copy this survey and give it to at least one confidant who knows you well personally and one coworker who knows you in action and who agree to answer the questions frankly about you. You could interview the respondent, but he or she would probably be more comfortable working on this without having to look you in the eye. Point out to your helpers that "our hero" refers to you. Fill out a copy yourself. After you collect their work, you'll compare information among the two or more sets of responses and then reorganize those data into a description of a good position for you.

1.   What is the accomplishment in her or his work in the last two years that our hero is most proud of? Why is our hero so proud of this accomplishment?

2.   Describe a mistake our hero made recently in his or her work life and what he or she learned from it.

3.   Give two examples of jobs our hero would hold even after she or he won the lottery.

   1.

   2.

4. Name the talents our hero exhibits in his or her pastimes.

5. Describe an experience in the last year in which our hero acquired or sharpened a competence, skill, or ability.

6. Name two specific courses our hero most enjoyed in college.

   1.

   2.

7. Name two places our hero would like to live when she or he finishes the degree.

   1.

2.

8. Name a job or career our hero has expressed an interest in recently.

9. How many hours a week does our hero seem likely to devote to his or her job?
   - ❏ less than 30
   - ❏ 30–39
   - ❏ 40–49
   - ❏ 50–59
   - ❏ 60 or more

10. What would our hero like for a starting salary?

11. Our hero prefers to work . . . (check one)
    - ❏ self-employed
    - ❏ in a small, mobile, but probably less stable organization
    - ❏ in a large, stable organization

12. Our hero prefers working conditions of . . . (check one or two)

    ❑ doing tasks independently

    ❑ working in small teams of equals with varied specialties

    ❑ assisting a supervisor or director

    ❑ partnering with another in the same field

    ❑ acting as a go-between among a mix of organizations,
      clients, workers

13. Name an activity our hero has enjoyed in his or her job (or recent job).

14. Describe two weaknesses in our hero's academic performance.

    1.

    2.

15. Name two strengths in our hero's academic work.

    1.

2.

16. How important to our hero is each of the following in her or his job goals?

Job characteristic	Our hero would rate this as ...			
Big salary	important	a little	not important	don't know
Health insurance and retirement benefits	important	a little	not important	don't know
Doing good for the world	important	a little	not important	don't know
Solving problems	important	a little	not important	don't know
Inventing something	important	a little	not important	don't know
Teamwork	important	a little	not important	don't know
Affecting policy and behavior	important	a little	not important	don't know
Public respect	important	a little	not important	don't know
Travel and adventure	important	a little	not important	don't know
Indoor work	important	a little	not important	don't know
Low stress	important	a little	not important	don't know
Intellectual work	important	a little	not important	don't know

(continued)

Job characteristic	*Our hero would rate this as ...*			
Serving and helping clients	important	a little	not important	don't know
Being measured and rewarded for success	important	a little	not important	don't know
Secure position	important	a little	not important	don't know
Frequent change of task	important	a little	not important	don't know
Directing others	important	a little	not important	don't know
Frequent change of coworkers	important	a little	not important	don't know
Job satisfying family expectations	important	a little	not important	don't know

THE REPORT

1. On your copy of the questionnaire, and in another color, add the answers from your respondents. Compare your answers to those of your respondents. Make a list below of the areas of greatest agreement and disagreement.

Agreement   *Disagreement*

2. How do you explain the main differences?

3. After reflecting on these results, describe your self-image (about a hundred words).

4. Based on this self-image, describe a good work setting and tasks in which you'll be satisfied and effective (about a hundred words).

Answers to
"What Were Their Majors?" (p. 2)

The occupational titles on the left were held by recent SUNY Potsdam graduates with the majors on the right.

Banking assistant manager	English
Child disability learning specialist	Biology
Physical education center instructor	Anthropology
Conservation officer	Anthropology
Stock market analyst	Music
Newspaper reporter	English, History, Philosophy
Paralegal professional	Chemistry

Works Cited

Note: You will find another good bibliography in *Getting a Job Outside the Academy* (see the first entry below). Although primarily designed for graduate students and professionals, that bibliography offers much to the undergraduate as well. It lists general employment manuals and guides; information on and examples of résumés and interviews; information on government jobs, organizations, employers, job opportunities; and directories of anthropologists.

American Anthropological Association (AAA). *Getting a Job Outside the Academy.* Washington, DC: AAA, 1982.

————. *Guide to Departments of Anthropology.* Arlington, VA: AAA (annual).

American Association of Physical Anthropologists. "A Career in Biological Anthropology." No date. Pamphlet available from the association's executive committee; inquire at *www.physanth.org.*

American Federation of Teachers. "The Employment Picture for Recent Grads." *On Campus* (September 1997): 2.

Anderson, Barbara Gallatin. *First Fieldwork.* Prospect Heights, IL: Waveland Press, 1992.

Baba, Marietta. *Business and Industrial Anthropology.* NAPA bulletin 2. Washington, DC: NAPA/AAA, 1986.

————. "The Fifth Subdiscipline: Anthropological Practice and the Future of Anthropology." *Human Organization* 53, no. 2 (1994): 174–86.

Barone, Timi. "Practical Advice from Practicing Anthropologists." *Anthropology Newsletter* (March 1999): 37–38.

Bestor, Dorothy. *Aside from Teaching, What in the World Can You Do?* Seattle: University of Washington Press, 1982.

Bird, S. Elizabeth, and Carolena Von Trapp. "Beyond Bones and Stones." *Anthropology News* (December 1999): 9–10.

Blum, Laurie. *Free Money for Graduate School,* 4th ed. New York: Facts on File, 2000.

Bolles, Richard Nelson. *What Color Is Your Parachute? 2000.* Berkeley: Ten Speed Press, 1999.

Boyd, Varna. Presentation at "Careers in Anthropology," sponsored by Anthropological Society of Washington, Anthropological Students Association, and University of Maryland, College Park, MD. December 5, 1998.

Briggs, John, and F. David Peat. *Seven Life Lessons of Chaos.* New York: HarperPerennial, 2000.

Briody, Elizabeth. "Profiles of Practice: Anthropological Careers in Business, Government, and Private Sector Associations." In *Anthropology for Tomorrow,* ed. Robert T. Trotter, 76–89. Washington, DC: NAPA/AAA, 1988.

Bronitsky, Gordon. "American Indians, World Markets: The Evolution of a Career."
    Practicing Anthropology 21, no. 1 (1999): 32–34.

Bush, David R. "The Incorporation of Cultural Resource Management into Academia."
    Cultural Resource Research, Report no. 2. Case Western Reserve University, Cleve-
    land, OH, April 16, 1981.

Chambers, Erve. "Career Guides for Anthropologists." *American Anthropologist* 86, no.
    3 (June 1984): 337–40.

Cohen, Robert. "There's More to a Name." *Stanford Business School Magazine* 63, no.
    3 (1995).

Conniff, James C. G. "Career Options: Is College Major a Major Factor?" *CPC Journal*
    12, no. 1 (Fall 1986): 48–52.

Corner, Brian D., and Claire C. Gordon. "Applied Physical Anthropology in the U.S.
    Army." *Practicing Anthropology* 18, no. 2 (1996): 10–13.

Cushing, Steven. *Fatal Words: Communication Clashes and Airplane Crashes.* Chicago:
    University of Chicago, 1993.

Davis, Nancy Yaw, Roger McConochie, and David R. Stevensen. *Research and Con-
    sulting as a Business,* NAPA bulletin 4. Washington, DC: NAPA/AAA, 1987.

Dettwyler, Katherine. *Dancing Skeletons.* Prospect Heights, IL: Waveland Press, 1994.

Donnelly, James H., Jr., James L. Gibson, and John M. Ivancevich. *Fundamentals of
    Management,* 8th ed. Homewood, IL: Irwin Publishers, 1992.

Dreyfus Corporation. *Third Century Fund Semiannual Report.* December 18, 1998.

Evans, Patsy. "AAA's Biennial Survey of Anthropology Ph.D.s: Career Trends." *Anthro-
    pology Newsletter* (November 1997): 6.

Figler, Howard. *The Complete Job-Search Handbook,* rev. ed. New York: Owl Books,
    1999.

Fillmore, Randolph. "Ph.D. Survey Results: 1988 Doctor Rate Update." *Anthropology
    Newsletter* (March 1989): 32.

Fiske, Shirley, and Erve Chambers. "The Inventions of Practice." *Human Organiza-
    tion* 55, no. 1 (1996): 1–12.

Foltz, Kim. "New Species for Study: Consumers in Action." *New York Times,* Novem-
    ber 18, 1989, D1.

Fowler, Don D., and Donald L. Hardesty, eds. *Others Viewing Others: The Ethno-
    graphic Career.* Washington, DC: Smithsonian Press, 1994.

Giovannini, Maureen, and Lynne M. H. Rosansky. *Anthropology and Management
    Consulting,* NAPA bulletin 9. Washington, DC: NAPA/AAA, 1990.

Givens, David B. *State Job Opportunities for Anthropologists.* Washington, DC: Ameri-
    can Anthropological Association, 1986.

———. "1996 Anthropology Careers." *Academic Relations Bulletin* 18, no. 2 (January
    1996): 1.

Givens, David B., Patsy Evans, and Timothy Jablonski. "1997 Survey of Anthropology
    Ph.D.s." In *Guide to Departments, 1997–1998,* 308–21. Arlington, VA: American
    Anthropological Association, 1997.

Goodman, Charity, and Liane Rosenblatt. "Applied Anthropologists and the Job Mar-
    ket: Strategies for Attaining Employment." Paper delivered at American Anthropo-
    logical Association annual conference. Washington, DC, 1991.

Greengrass, Mara. "Short Step to the Business World." *Anthropology News* (October
    1999a): 34–35.

———. "Media Monitor." *Anthropology News* (November 1999b): 28.

———. "Sidetracked by Aliens." *Anthropology News* (December 1999c): 28.

Guerron-Montero, Carla. "Student Column." *SfAA Newsletter* 8, no. 2 (May 1998): 7–8.

Hanson, Karen J., John J. Conway, Jack Alexander, H. Max Drake, eds. *Mainstreaming Anthropology: Experiences in Government Employment,* NAPA bulletin 5. Washington, DC: American Anthropological Association, 1988.

Heller, Scott. "From Selling Rambo to Supermarket Studies, Anthropologists Are Finding More Non-Academic Jobs." *Chronicle of Higher Education* 34, no. 38 (June 1, 1988): 3.

Hersh, Richard. "Intentions and Perceptions: A National Survey of Public Attitudes toward Liberal Arts Education." *Change* (March/April 1997): 16–23.

Hume, Ivor Noel. *Martin's Hundred: The Discovery of a Lost Colonial Virginia Settlement.* New York: Delta, 1982.

Hyland, Stanley, and Sean Kirkpatrick, eds. *Guide to Training Programs in the Applications of Anthropology,* 4th ed. Oklahoma City, OK: Society for Applied Anthropology, 1994.

Institute for Food and Development Policy. *Education for Action: Graduate Studies with a Focus on Social Change.* San Francisco: Food First Books, 1991.

Johnson, Nancy, ed. *NAPA Directory of Practicing Anthropologists.* Washington, DC: NAPA/AAA, 1991.

Jones, Del. "Hot Asset in Corporate: Anthropology Degrees." *USA Today,* February 18, 1999, B1.

Klein, Frederick C. "Research Probes Consumers Using Anthropological Skills." *Wall Street Journal,* July 7, 1983, 25.

Kratts, Aimee, and Clarissa Hunter. "Undergraduate Alumni Survey Results." *Anthropology Newsletter* (November 1986): 20.

Kuehnast, Kathleen. "Career Options Outside the Academy." *Anthropology News* (February 1999): 32.

Levy, Elaine. *College, Knowledge, and Jobs.* Albany: New York State Department of Labor, 1991.

Malnig, Lawrence R., and Anita Malnig. *What Can I Do with a Major in . . . ? How to Choose and Use Your College Major.* Ridgefield, NJ: Abbott Press, 1984.

McCurdy, David W., and Donna F. Carlson. "The Shrink-wrap Solution: Anthropology in Business." In *Conformity and Conflict,* ed. James Spradley and David McCurdy, 233–45. Boston: Little, Brown, 1984.

Meaney, F. J. "Across the Parking Lot and into Public Health Again." *Practicing Anthropology* 7, no. 3 (1995): 10.

Moffatt, Michael. *Coming of Age in New Jersey.* Brunswick, NJ: Rutgers University Press, 1986.

Nadler, Burton. *Liberal Arts Power: What It Is and How to Sell It on Your Résumé,* 2d ed. Princeton, NJ: Peterson's, 1989a.

———. *Liberal Arts Jobs: Where They Are and How to Get Them,* 2d ed. Princeton, NJ: Peterson's, 1989b.

Neely, Sharlotte. "Career Choice in Anthropology." In *Let's Go Anthropology: Travels on the Internet,* ed. Joan Ferrante, 157–60. New York: Wadsworth, 1998.

Neuhauser, Peg. *Tribal Warfare in Organizations.* New York: HarperBusiness, 1990.

———. *Corporate Legends and Lore.* Burr Ridge, IL: McGraw-Hill, 1993.

Newman, Sven, ed. *So, What Are You Doing After College?* New York: Henry Holt and Co., 1995.

Oakes, Dallin, ed. *Linguistics at Work: A Reader of Applications.* Orlando, FL: Harcourt Brace and Co., 1998.

Okrand, Marc. "Nouns (A Chapter Excerpt from *The Klingon Dictionary*)." In *Linguistics at Work: A Reader of Applications,* ed. Dallin Oakes, 196–208. Fort Worth, TX: Harcourt Brace and Co., 1998.

Overbey, Peggy. "Policy Monitor." *Anthropology News* (November 1999): 27.

Peterson's staff. *Peterson's Grants for Graduate and Postdoctoral Study,* 4th ed. Princeton, NJ: Peterson's Guides, 1995.

Peterson's staff. *Peterson's Guide to Graduate and Professional Programs,* vol. 1–6, 33rd ed. Princeton, NJ: Peterson's Guides, 1999.

Podolevsky, Aaron, and Peter Brown, eds. *Applying Anthropology.* Mountain View, CA: Mayfield Publishing, 1999.

Powdermaker, Hortense. *Stranger and Friend.* New York: W. W. Norton, 1966.

Raybeck, Douglas. *Looking Down the Road.* Prospect Heights, IL: Waveland Press, 2000.

Reich, Robert. "The Two Great Forces of the Future." In *World Almanac 2000,* 33–34. Mahwah, NJ: Primedia Reference, 1999.

Ruiz, Carmen Garcia. "Toolkit for Professional Anthropologists." *Anthropology News* (March 2000): 44–45.

Ryan, Alan, ed. *A Guide to Careers in Physical Anthropology.* Westport, CT: Greenwood Press, 2000.

Schwimmer, Brian E., and D. Michael Warren, eds. *Anthropology and the Peace Corps: Case Studies in Career Preparation.* Iowa City: Iowa State University Press, 1993.

Singer, Merrill, ed. *Anthropologists at Work: Responses to Student Questions about Anthropology Careers.* Arlington, VA: NAPA/AAA, 1994.

Smithsonian Institution. *Museum Studies International: A Directory of Museum Training Programs in the U.S. and Abroad.* Washington, DC: Smithsonian Institution (annual).

Spradley, James P. "Career Education in Cultural Perspective." In *Essays on Career Education,* ed. Larry McClure and Carolyn Buan, 3–16. Portland, OR: Northwest Regional Educational Laboratory (U.S. Office of Education), 1973.

SUNY Potsdam Career Planning Office. *Career Opportunity News,* October 1997.

———. *Faculty Newsbytes,* January 1998, September 1998, January 1999, September 1999, Spring 2000.

SUNY Potsdam Office of Career Services. *SUNY Career Services Annual Report, 1989–90.* Potsdam: SUNY Potsdam, 1990.

Tannen, Deborah. "The Power of Talk: Who Gets Heard and Why." *Harvard Business Review* (September-October 1995).

Tefft, Stanton, with Cathy Harris and Glen Godwin. "North Carolina Undergraduate Alumni Survey." *Anthropology Newsletter* (January 1988): 28.

Textor, Robert. *A Handbook on Ethnographic Futures Research.* Stanford, CA: Stanford University School of Education and Department of Anthropology, 1980.

Trotter, Robert. *Anthropology for Tomorrow,* special publication 24. Washington, DC: NAPA/AAA, 1988.

Ubelaker, Douglas, and Henry Scammell. *Bones: A Forensic Detective's Casebook.* New York: HarperCollins, 1992.

Useem, Michael. *Liberal Education and the Corporation: The Hiring and Advancement of College Graduates.* Chicago: Aldine de Gruyter, 1989.

Vahle-Hamel, April, Mary Morris-Heiberger, and Julia Miller-Vick. *Graduate School Funding Handbook.* Philadelphia: University of Pennsylvania Press, 1995.

Van Willigen, John. *Becoming a Practicing Anthropologist: A Guide to Careers and Training Programs in Applied Anthropology,* NAPA bulletin no. 3. Washington, DC: NAPA/AAA, 1987.

Van Willigen, John, Barbara Rylko-Bauer, and Ann McElroy, eds. *Making Our Research Useful: Case Studies in the Utilization of Anthropological Knowledge.* Boulder, CO: Westview, 1989.

Ward, R., and F. J. Meaney. "Anthropometry and Numerical Taxonomy in Clinical Genetics." *American Journal of Physical Anthropology* 64, no. 1 (1995): 147–54.

Weatherford, Jack. *Tribes on the Hill: The U.S. Congress Rituals and Realities,* rev. ed. New York: Bergen and Garvey, 1985.

Wienker, Curtis W. "Career Alternatives for Physical Anthropologists." *Practicing Anthropology* 4, no. 3 (1991): 27–30.

———. "Physical Anthropology and Biomedical Careers." *Practicing Anthropology* 5, no. 3 (1993): 20–21.

Wulff, Robert, and Shirley Fiske, eds. *Anthropological Praxis.* Boulder, CO: Westview, 1987.

Zeder, Melinda. *The American Archaeologist: A Profile.* Thousand Oaks, CA: Altamira Press, 1997.

SOME USEFUL PERIODICALS

AnthroNotes

A Museum of Natural History Publication for Educators. Available free to teachers. Contact Ruth Selig, Editor, Anthropology Outreach Office, National Museum of Natural History, Washington, DC 20560-0112; e-mail: selig.ruth@nmnh.si.edu.

Anthropology News

Newsletter published ten times a year. Available free to members of the American Anthropological Association. Contact Susan Skomal, American Anthropological Association, 4350 N. Fairfax Dr., Suite 640, Arlington, VA 22203-1620; telephone 703-528-1902, ext. 3005; e-mail: sskomal@aaanet.org.

Aviso

Monthly newsletter of the American Association of Museums (AAM). Available free to members of AAM or for $40 per year. The focus is current news and professional development; job announcements are published. AAM also publishes the monthly *Museum News,* which focuses on museum activities such as curation and acquisitions. Available free to members or for $38 per year. Previewed on the Web at *www. aam-us.org/pubp.htm.*

Common Ground

Federal government archaeology magazine. Contact Editor, NPS Archaeology and Ethnography Program, 1849 C St. (NC 210) NW, Washington, DC 20240; telephone 202-343-4101; e-mail: david_andrews@nps.gov.

CRM

Federal government cultural resource management magazine. Contact U.S. Department of the Interior, National Park Service, Cultural Resources, P.O. Box 37127, Washington, DC 20013-7127; telephone 202-343-3395; e-mail: ron_greenberg@nps.gov.

General Anthropology

Newsletter available free to members of General Anthropology Division of AAA. Contact Patricia Rice, Department of Sociology and Anthropology, West Virginia University, Morgantown, WV 26506; telephone 304-293-5801; e-mail: price@wvu.edu.

Physical Anthropology Newsletter

Available on the Internet at *www.physanth.org/newsletter/physanthnews.html*.

Practicing Anthropology

Newsletter available free to members of Society for Applied Anthropology (SfAA). Contact Alexander M. Ervin, Department of Anthropology and Archaeology, 55 Campus Drive, University of Saskatchewan, Saskatoon, Saskatchewan, S7N 5B1 Canada; telephone 306-966-4176; e-mail: ervin@sask.usask.ca.

SAA Bulletin

Society for American Archaeology. Available on the Internet at *www.anth.ucsb.edu/ SAABulletin*.

SfAA Newsletter

Available free to members of SfAA. Contact Michael B. Whiteford, Department of Anthropology, 324 Curtiss Hall, Iowa State University, Ames, IA 50011-1050; telephone 515-294-8212; e-mail: jefe@iastate.edu.

The Nation's Health

A monthly newsletter of the American Public Health Association (APHA). Available free to members of APHA or for $30 per year for eleven issues. More information available at *www.apha.org/journal/nation/tnhhome.htm*. Contact American Public Health Association, Subscriptions, Box 5037, Washington, DC 20061-5037.

Index

Note: Page numbers in *italic* refer to figures; those in **boldface** refer to tables. Page numbers followed by n refer to footnotes.

157